25

DEFINITIVE NEW ORLEANS RESTAURANTS

(& A DOZEN DAMNED GOOD PLACES TO DRINK)

ONE NOVELIST'S NOTES ON A 40-YEAR SPREE
OF GLUTTONY & GUZZLING
Written Without Reservations by
Steven Wells Hicks

2015 Edition

Fiction by Steven Wells Hicks

The Gleaner
The Fall of Adam
Horizontal Adjustment
Destiny's Anvil

ISBN-13: 978-1505655834
ISBN-10: 1505655838
To query about permissions for advertising and/or other text usage,
please contact the author at hickswrites@gmail.com

For forty years, I've been chasing the essence of New Orleans through countless restaurants, roadhouses, bistros, beaneries and bars.

This is what I've learned.

Try as you might, you'll never find the "true" New Orleans.

That's because there isn't just one.

People come to the Crescent City for all kinds of reasons, and sooner or later the city obliges. Some people come out of sheer curiosity; others to satisfy their cultural, culinary or even carnal appetites. Most go home smiling.

New Orleans can be particularly challenging to the food-oriented visitor due to the city's variety of homegrown offerings. As the port city separating the great American breadbasket from the world at large, New Orleans has served as a culinary melting pot of ingredients, techniques and peoples for nearly 300 years. The result is a distinct, indigenous style of cooking that has grown not so much out of a collision but rather a conglomeration of cultures and cooking methods from around the globe.

Consider gumbo, perhaps the most iconic New Orleans food. Its name comes from the Western Africa word for okra. Its base is a classic French roux adopted by Creoles of mixed Spanish and African descent. The andouille sausage and chicken variety of the dish incorporates traditional Cajun livestock. Seafood gumbo features shrimp, crab and oysters, a commodity once controlled by Slovenian fishermen and now largely harvested by second- and third-generation Vietnamese immigrants. Sicilians added their traditional aromatics and locally cultivated produce to the pot, which was originally seasoned with spice blends concocted by Caribbean slaves of African origin. The final result is widely considered an all-American favorite.

The idea of a "real" New Orleans cuisine becomes more elusive when you consider the city has her foot in three different centuries, and the pace of culinary evolution is constantly accelerating.

This guidebook was developed for visitors to the Crescent City more interested in getting a taste of traditional New Orleans cuisine than they might be in food with its foundation in the latest fad or foible. That's not to say visitors in search of more aggressive, au courant cooking or food from a broader range of nations than those most typically associated with the city can't find either in Greater New Orleans. You just won't find them included in this particular book.

For example, I am partial to Saffron NOLA, a little-known Indian restaurant that only serves dinner on Fridays in a dilapidated suburban strip center across the Mississippi River on the West Bank. But the vast majority of travelers don't come to New Orleans for Indian fare any more than they'd fly to New Delhi for a roast beef poor boy sandwich dripping with gravy. Consequently, Saffron NOLA, is nowhere to be found in this book except within this paragraph.

Since it's sometimes easier to describe a guidebook by what's not in it than what is, let me add that you won't find any franchise restaurants in this book – not only the national megabrands like Popeye's Chicken & Biscuits and Ruth's Chris Steak House, both of which originated in the Crescent City, but also operations that started in New Orleans and have branched out with more than five restaurants. This takes out Emeril Lagasse and his dozen restaurants from coast-to-coast, John Besh's multiple operations (although Sunday brunch at LaProvence on the north shore of Lake Ponchartrain remains a personal favorite) and all the restaurants that make up the Brennan family's sprawling restaurant empire.

One of the things that has allowed New Orleans to evolve into an American culinary capital is its adherence to the notion of a restaurant as a place where a single family grows and works together, at least until the family has grown enough to consider opening a second location because all those relatives have outgrown the original premises.

The definitive case in point could very well be the descendants of Antoine Alciatore who still own and operate the city's oldest restaurant, Antoine's, dating back to 1840. Now in its 175th year of operation, Antoine's remains a single restaurant on St. Louis Street, although it has grown to fifteen rooms interconnected in a labyrinthine pattern taking up the better half of a city block.

As much as anything, this book could be called a cleaned-up collection of notes made over forty years of searching for the elusive heart and spirit of a city that has become equally legendary for its restaurants as its history as the cradle of jazz.

While the quality of the cuisines to be found certainly occupy the metaphoric driver's seat of the essays found within, this book is also a vehicle to talk about other factors that make dining in New Orleans such a singular experience: a restaurant's history, its ambiance, how signature dishes were created and developed or even the occasional intangible "X-factor" that makes the establishment both integral and indigenous to the city.

You see, at the heart of every traditional New Orleans restaurant and saloon is a story waiting to be told and, as a novelist by trade, that is as irresistible to me a perfectly cooked crawfish etouffée.

Ultimately this book is a valentine, sometimes left-handed but hopefully right-minded, to a city and the people of an industry that have simultaneously provided me with a lifetime of sensuous fulfillment while wreaking untold havoc with my waistline and the balance on my American Express card.

So exactly how many "definitive" restaurants are there in the Greater New Orleans area? One local blogger and radio host, Tom Fitzmorris, publishes a list of 350 "essential restaurants," which amount to roughly one-quarter of the total number of true restaurants he follows in the city.

The decision to limit the contents of this guidebook is perhaps arbitrary but was not reached by a belief that there are only 25 definitive restaurants and a dozen good saloons in the city. There are certainly more. The reasons for such a limitation, however, are twofold:

First, I wanted to list restaurants where the odds are strong that you'll get a better than good meal in a place that will usually provide you with not only a pleasurable experience but also a taste of the spirit of this remarkable city.

Second, in order to provide you with more than a glorified telephone directory sprinkled with capricious star ratings, I've written at a leisurely length in an attempt to give you more background and insight, to set the table if you will, before you settle in to a meal bearing the promise of remaining unforgettable for years to come.

Ultimately, any book of commentary on restaurants and food is subjective and reflects the tastes, opinion and even the prejudices of its author. This collection of essays and observations is based upon personal opinion. I don't expect you to agree with me on everything, because when all is said and done, none of us are anything more than a man or woman with a knife and a fork.

Bon appétit, mes amis.

THE CLASSICS

Every great city has a handful of restaurants that somehow manage to lift themselves beyond the day-to-day operations of certain successful enterprises to become virtual signatures for the city itself.

The rooms can be as elegant as The Four Seasons in New York or as unassuming as Swan Oyster Depot in San Francisco. The food can be as pedigreed as that served at Bocuse in Lyons or as uncomplicated as a platter of stone crab claws at Joe's in Miami.

It wasn't so long ago that New Orleans had six "name" restaurants, know collectively as les grande dames. They were Antoine's, Arnaud's, Brennan's, Broussard's, Commander's Palace and Galatoire's. Well, times pass and temples crumble. Brennan's went belly up in 2012, only to re-open, re-invented in the closing days of 2014. In 2013, Broussard's was sold, and a new group came in and are trying to regain the restaurant's lost luster. Antoine's, the oldest family-operated restaurant in the United States, and Commander's Palace have slipped from their long-held pedestals as the city's two top restaurants. Whether they are victims of a changing world or are refusing to change along with it is a matter of opinion. Just the same, it's sad to see some of the grand ladies lose a step.

The truth is, however, that New Orleans has always had more classic restaurants than the six grande dames. Their fame may not have spread as far, their food may not be French Creole, they may not all have French Quarter addresses and their rooms may not look like they belong in museums.

What they have in common are loyal customers whose families have been coming to the restaurants for generations. The "newcomer" of the six restaurants selected as classics for this book is Willie Mae's Scotch House, which dates back to 1957, when Willie Mae Seaton opened a saloon in a dicey part of the city and grew it into a tiny restaurant with a big national reputation for fried chicken.

To become a classic takes more than hanging around for over half a century. The food served today will have changed little since the restaurants opened their doors. Some tinkering has taken place with the recipes and techniques to accommodate improvements in both, but the food remains remarkably faithful to its origins.

The idea of New Orleans as one of America's culinary capitals is hardly new. These six classic restaurants still represent six building blocks of that enviable reputation.

Galatoire's

All said, it is a room more accommodating to easy conversation than stiff formality,
a place conducive to deciding the world will be better served
with one more bottle of champagne than three more hours of work.

Sometimes events occur close enough to each other that they lead people to suspect there must be some cause-and-effect relationship between them.

Lately, I've found myself pondering the possible linkage of two seemingly incongruent facts. The first is the 1905 opening of Jean Galatoire's bistro in the building that had already housed Victor's restaurant for 75 years. The second occurred two years later, when an enterprising tailor around the corner from the bistro cut and stitched together the first two-piece seersucker suit.

While common sense leads to the inevitable conclusion that the seersucker suit was designed to offer gentlemen a fashionable respite from the subtropical heat and brutal humidity of a New Orleans summer, I might consider a good-natured wager that the chap who purchased that original blue and white seersucker suit made a beeline from the tailor's shop to his standing Friday lunch at Galatoire's — and that five generations later, his great-great-great grandson is likely doing the same.

To declare Galatoire's the finest opportunity to experience the charm, grace and esprit of New Orleans is no stretch. If anything, it's predictable, perhaps even inescapable, but the reason for the restaurant's continuing acclaim is at once unusual, ephemeral and one of the most cherished attributes of the city herself.

The success of most restaurants is based upon the food they serve,

11

yet any number of New Orleans eateries can lay claim to more innovative recipes and presentations than those that have been coming out of the Galatoire's kitchen for over one hundred years. While some establishments base their success on the glittering reputations of up-and-coming superstar chefs, more than a century of chefs and line cooks have toiled in relative obscurity, if not outright anonymity, at Galatoire's. Moreover, few local residents would quibble with the contention that numerous dining rooms exist in the city where the décor is more romantic or refined, and the service is less daunting.

So what is the element, the sine qua non, which lifts Galatoire's to its lofty status as arguably the city's signature restaurant?

In a word, continuity.

On those rare occasions when Galatoire's management allows change to occur at all, the slightest alteration is undertaken with great trepidation. Even the most miniscule modification will be met with a chorus of harrumphs and howls of outrage from hidebound regulars who regard any break with tradition as the hand basket in which the world is being carted off to Hell.

As a result, the front doors at Galatoire's have become and remain a final barricade against a world that has become faster, harsher and increasingly ill-mannered; a last bastion of both gentility and the camaraderie of neighborly table-hopping between people who renew their friendships on a weekly basis.

Step out the doors, outside this coddling cocoon where champagne flutes clink and patrician waiters gently nudge patrons toward the day's freshest offerings, and you're sucked into the maelstrom of Bourbon Street with its jaded bump-and-grind of topless clubs, condom shops, clip joints, t-shirt emporia, fluorescent drinks, hot dog stands and teeming flocks of slack-jawed yokels taking it all in.

In 1911, when Jean Galatoire paid $25,000 for the building that houses his restaurant, it was shoehorned between a laundry and a genteel dress shop. The Storyville District, where jazz was born and sporting girls plied their trade in everything from Gilded Age parlors to clapboard cribs, was blocks away across Basin Street. Bourbon Street was still a setting where upright citizens needn't turn red-faced should they bump into their priests or preachers.

For over a century, Galatoire's has emphatically refused to move, or change very much of anything for that matter. The restaurant nearly doubled its size, however, in 2013 with the addition of the "33" Bar and an adjacent steakhouse room in a Katrina-abandoned building next door. Despite the expansion, the Galatoire's of today remains a tea rose atop a dung pile, a prince among frogs, a cherished Degas painting in a posterized Andy Warhol world.

From all appearances, Galatoire's has never noticed the transition of Bourbon Street. Indeed, the restaurant quietly goes about its business, does things in its own long-established ways and, on its 100th anniversary in 2005, was cited as the Outstanding Restaurant in the nation in the prestigious James Beard Foundation awards.

Consider the world as it was one hundred years before in 1905, when the restaurant's new owner was cutting the ropes used to display smoked hams and game in the storefront windows of Victor Bero's 75 year-old bistro, and nailing up the sign that would evermore designate the building at 209 Bourbon Street as Galatoire's.

Theodore Roosevelt was living in the building he renamed "The White House." Ragtime was all the musical rage. In Pittsburgh, the death knell sounded for the nickelodeon when the first modern movie theater opened to packed houses spellbound by the flickering fourteen-minute Western, The Great Train Robbery. It was the year Albert Einstein reinvented physics with the simple formula $e=mc2$, Ernest Hemingway was a schoolboy and a woman could still get two cents back after buying a quart of milk for a dime.

The earth has logged over 40,000 rotations since Galatoire's opened is doors. America has fought six wars and been led by eighteen presidents. Rock steady in the swirling winds of history, Galatoire's has managed to change hardly at all.

Yes, there have been adjustments, small concessions to unstoppable progress and changing tastes. Air conditioning ultimately replaced fans blowing across ice blocks. Neckties for gentlemen became no longer required, but any man without a jacket after five or anytime Sunday can expect to be offered a coat from the foyer rack, or graciously escorted back through the front doors and once again to the sidewalk of Bourbon Street. After ninety years as a cash-only establishment, the restaurant finally gave in several years ago and started to begrudgingly accept credit cards.

A 1999 renovation moved the front doors to a side foyer and eliminated the airlock that partially shielded Tennessee Williams' regular table from public view, thereby allowing the eccentric playwright to indulge in catty gossip or snipe at other diners entering or leaving the room.

After a suitable period of agonized hand-wringing and teeth gnashing, most changes are eventually accepted by Galatoire's regulars with a certain amount of aplomb, but not always. When a popular waiter was fired after being sued for sexual harassment, enraged regulars wrote such incendiary letters to The Times-Picayune that a local theatrical troupe assembled them into an hour-long play. Management's decision to install a mechanical ice shaver, thereby ending the time-honored practice of having employees chip ice by hand, caused customer rumblings about a narrowly avoided mutiny of Potemkin proportions.

Resistance to change is so fervently embraced by both the owners and regular customers of Galatoire's that their relationship has emerged as irrevocably symbiotic. The celebration of all things status quo is even reflected in the restaurant's extensive menu, where it is far easier to find a traditional French-Creole offering dating back to 1905 than to find one that doesn't.

An item has to fall so far out of culinary favor to be removed from the wide-ranging menu that very few have ever been, giving the bistro a quaint charm with the occasional inclusion of items like sheepshead, a flat-toothed fish that looks far more appealing on a plate than the bony thing ever did in the sea.

New additions to the menu come equally slowly. Consider two items that have become New Orleans standards that are yet to appear on Galatoire's menu. It's been more than thirty years since Paul Prudhomme launched a national craze for Louisiana cooking with blackened redfish from K-Paul's on Chartres Street. Drago's signature charbroiled oysters made their first appearance at the Cvitanovitch family's Metairie restaurant in 1993 and have since been knocked off by dozens of local places. Neither dish is yet to grace the pages of the lengthy Galatoire's menu.

Most new items to appear on the menu have been created in the Galatoire's kitchen by either staff or members of the Galatoire family, some of whom continue to work with the restaurant despite the sale of its majority interest in 2010. Crabmeat Yvonne was named for the founder's granddaughter, who started working behind the cashier's desk when a regular worker called in sick in 1938 and eventually became the company's president, serving until her death in 2000. It is a simple dish, five sautéed ingredients that can be presented as either a main course or prepared as a garnish for any number of entrées.

The Godchaux Salad was named after Leon Godchaux, who in the 1920s would walk to lunch at Galatoire's daily from his fashionable department store on nearby Canal Street. During the scorching summer heat, the merchant would request a salad made from his favorite ingredients — iceberg lettuce, boiled shrimp, lump crabmeat, anchovies and vine-ripened tomatoes with a Creole mustard vinaigrette. Today, ninety years later, the salad is still a mainstay on the menu.

One of the restaurant's signature appetizers, the Crabmeat Canapé Lorenzo, was named after the neighborhood pharmacist. Jumbo lump crabmeat is folded into a traditional Béchamel sauce with scallions, parsley, butter, egg yolks and seasoned with butter and both white and cayenne pepper. The mixture is next coated with breadcrumbs and grated Parmesan, and then spread on a toast round. Finally, anchovy filets are criss-crossed on top and finished to an earthy brown in the broiler.

The vast majority of the cuisine served at Galatoire's has its roots in the fundamentals of French or Creole cooking, which the restaurant has merged over the years into the hybrid they call, not surprisingly, French Creole. Because of New Orleans' location near the Gulf of Mexico, there is a natural emphasis on fish and shellfish, but that certainly doesn't preclude the same attention paid – and creativity applied – to a panoply of meat, game, poultry and even egg dishes.

Like the restaurant itself, the food is time-tested and traditional rather than highly imaginative. It has been repeatedly prepared and adjusted to the point that the master recipes don't change because there's no longer any need.

Over the course of a century, foods originated by other restaurants have found their way onto the Galatoire's menu, most notably Oysters Rockefeller, crisp yet puffy soufflé potatoes and pompano en papillote, all created by Antoine's, the city's oldest extant restaurant dating back to 1840. When two restaurants share a combined 285 years of experience, it is expected that each will cultivate its own group of devotees, and when Antoine's regulars like to remind those from Galatoire's that a dish was invented at Antoine's, they can expect to hear the reply, "Yes, but it was perfected at Galatoire's."

While Galatoire's menu is both long and wide-ranging, an examination of the restaurant's elegant cookbook published in 2005 reveals that the recipes are simpler than one might expect, the cooking times quicker and the ingredient lists shorter. One of the core reasons for this, the restaurant freely admits, is the superiority of ingredients arriving daily from the legion of purveyors with whom Galatoire's has forged relationships now calculable in generations.

For well over a dozen years, Galatoire's has been operating on both the first and second floors of their original building at 209 Bourbon Street, the second floor having been reopened as part of the 1999 renovation. The second floor had been a colorful element of the restaurant's early years. A cluster of several small rooms referred to as les chambres privées, it had been used for private parties and, quite often, circumspect assignations for two. A private entrance and discreet staff kept downstairs clientele abuzz with conjecture regarding the identities and whispers about the activities taking place over their heads. The city's scandalmongers must have been heartbroken when the rooms closed during World War II. The upstairs rooms today are very public and the only part of the original restaurant that will accept reservations. They are rarely filled to capacity since the heart of Galatoire's is clearly the first-floor dining room below.

At first glance, the downstairs room looks as if it might have been plucked from a Parisian bistro circa 1900. Despite tuxedoed waiters and often impeccably dressed patrons, there is not what most people would describe as an air of elegance in the room.

The floors are tile, the chairs bent wood, the walls bedecked with curved brass coat hooks and large mirrors above panels of white wainscot. Above the mirrors is rich green wallpaper with gold fleur de lis hand stenciling. Twin-bladed fans lazily revolve from the ceiling.

In the back of the room, next to the kitchen entrance, a crisply dressed host or hostess surveys the scene from behind an antique cashier's station, above which is a tall pendulum clock that marks the passage of hours with its stately chime.

All said, it is a room more accommodating to easy conversation than stiff formality, a place conducive to deciding the world will be better served with one more bottle of champagne than three more hours at work. Despite the grand clock's chiming, there are few places better suited for paying no attention to time.

First-time visitors to Galatoire's would do well to remember one simple rule, which will assure a pleasurable and memorable experience: Trust your waiter. Some are as much of an institution at the restaurant as turtle soup or Poached Trout Margurey. Although their numbers have been diminishing through retirement or passing away, it wasn't all that long ago when seven members of one extended Cajun family worked the floor at the same time.

A waiter's position at Galatoire's is not a job, but rather a lucrative career to those who ply it. When asked, your waiter will quietly inform you of what looks best in the kitchen that particular day or may subtly shake his or her head should you order an item that might be better on another day. For visitors to whom the language of a French Creole kitchen is unfamiliar, the waiter can become an indispensable guide, explaining a dish or technique in such an affable manner it's difficult

17

to believe it's his ten thousandth time to do so.

While some visitors and guidebooks have referred to the corps working the front of the house as "condescending" or even "dictatorial," I have found their behavior to be a fairly accurate reflection of their patron. A cold or arrogant customer will be politely treated, of course, but with a chilling reserve. On the other hand, a guest who is friendly and curious will soon be treated like the newest member of an extended, happy family.

Regular guests soon request "their" waiter and the line separating server and those being served first blurs, then evaporates. My bride, hereinafter referred to as "The Sensible One," and I were fortunate enough to have one of the seven Cajun waiters, Louis LaFleur from Ville Plat, as "our" waiter for fifteen years. It didn't take long before, upon our entrance, Louis would arrive with a chilled bottle of Veuve Clicquot, a report on the supply and merit of the day's lump crabmeat, stories about his family and complaints about his aching feet. Until his passing, we referred to lunch at Galatoire's as "a visit with Louis."

While the restaurant's traditions rarely change, and then are merely tweaked, there is one tradition destined to stay in place for as long as the Galatoire name remains above the canopy. That tradition is "the line."

While the upstairs room now accepts reservations, the policy in the more desired downstairs remains no reservations, no exceptions. There is a famous story of former United States Senator J. Bennett Johnston being brought into the restaurant from deep in the line to accept a phone call from then President Ronald Reagan and upon the call's completion returning to his place in line.

There is another story I've heard numerous times with various names over the years, a story that's most likely apocryphal, but one that illustrates the restaurant's ironclad adherence to its policy. Legend has it that French president Charles de Gaulle was in New Orleans and appeared at Galatoire's door with an entourage. When politely told how happy the establishment was to see him but that he would need to take his place in line like everyone else, the former commander of the French army supposedly asked if the host knew who he was. "Oui, Monsieur President," the host is purported to have answered, "but do you know where you are?" The anecdote ends with de Gaulle storming away in a Gallic snit. Over the years, I've heard the names of the Duke of Windsor, William Randolph Hearst and others used in place of the French general, and I doubt the veracity of any of them, but people who know Galatoire's and its rules know just how believable such a scenario is.

In recent years, particularly in advance of the legendary Friday lunches, a regrettable practice has not only started, but flourished – the use of "placeholders" – people hired to spend Friday mornings standing in line so their employers can replace them five minutes before the doors open, thereby avoiding the need to endure a long wait like the commoners.

The fact that Galatoire's allows such an elitist system to survive is bewildering, at least to me. To the restaurant's defense, however, for the two busiest Fridays every year, those before Christmas and Fat Tuesday (Mardi Gras), Galatoire's has initiated auctions for tables and seating with proceeds going to local charities.

Friday lunches at Galatoire's have become a much written about tradition in New Orleans. During the summer months, you will see any number of men wearing seersucker or bow ties despite the loosened dress code. A handful of women will wear large, elegant hats, and air kisses will be blown from table to table as freely as doubloons are thrown at a Carnival parade. Martini glasses will clink, wine bottles will be uncorked in prodigious numbers, platters of food will cascade out of the kitchen and from time to time, a waiter will clink a knife against a water glass to announce birthdays and lead the entire room in song. It is not uncommon for the revelry to last all afternoon and often through dinner. This has led to an unofficial motto, "Come for lunch, stay for dinner, go home in a wheelbarrow."

From my point of view, however, Friday lunches at Galatoire's are an event that a visitor would be wiser to skip. Over the years, I've been to a healthy number of them. The food has been up to the high standard, the drinks icy, the service both friendly and crisp, and everyone as pleasant as they can be. But Fridays at Galatoire's are ultimately the province of clockwork regulars and insiders, a Petrie dish for social inbreeding New Orleans style. While visitors are certainly welcome, they will soon discover that the party swirls around them rather than includes them. They won't be on the outside looking in; they'll be on the inside looking in.

Some say Galatoire's has lost a step or two in the years since controlling interest in Galatoire's was sold to "outsiders." Perhaps it has, but any change is anathema to hardcore regulars whose families have patronized the bistro for generations. Death and retirement have taken their tolls on the group of patrician waiters who were always the true managers of Galatoire's, if not in title then certainly in essence. As New Orleans has become more laudatory of innovative chefs, the restaurant's unchanging cuisine has become described by some as dowdy rather than ageless. Such is the price paid when an establishment evolves into an institution, a last bastion of grace in a society that is always changing, but not necessarily for the better.

It is too early to tell if the new "33" bar or steakhouse room will enhance or dilute the rich history of Galatoire's.

No doubt I'm out of touch with the times, but I knew something was unsettling the first time The Sensible One and I walked into the elegant, new "33" saloon. It is a handsome room with its large wooden bar and love seats scattered throughout. A grand piano occupies a far corner. The martinis are crisp and cold enough to have ice crystals floating on the surface. The bartender was as affable as he was accomplished. It was TSO who first realized what was out of sync about "33." There are televisions in the room, at least four, a couple of them oversized, wall-mounted flat-screen models.

Forty years ago when I was a cub writer in an advertising agency, my mentor maintained, "No self-respecting saloon has ever been improved by the presence of a television set." While I'm not sure I agree in every case, the very idea of a television set in Galatoire's, with its rich traditions of civility, is somewhere between anathema and heresy. Should they possess the least bit of insight into what makes Galatoire's work, one can only hope management will regain its senses and toss the infernal things out the door to join their cultural counterparts on Bourbon Street.

Because of its relative newness and TSI's and my habit of letting new restaurants work out their kinks before we partake, we are yet to have dinner at the steakhouse. We peeked in to see what it looked like and, while the room itself seemed pleasant enough, to me it looked like someplace trying to be evocative of the original Galatoire's but coming up short. Preliminary reports from friends whose opinions we trust suggest that while the food itself is very good, there seems to be something incompatible between the essence of Galatoire's and the reality of a steakhouse.

For visitors wishing to absorb the whole Galatoire's experience, two elements are necessary; first, a mind open to the idea that newer isn't always better and, secondly, time itself.

If you let down your guard and open your heart to the original bistro, you will be transported back a century into the last unruffled days of America's gilded age, but such a journey requires the time to savor it. I believe the shortest lunch The Sensibele One (TSI) and I ever enjoyed at Galatoire's lasted slightly over two hours. The longest went from 11:30 in the morning until 5:45 that afternoon, entailed three bottles of Veuve, two Crabmeat Canapé Lorenzos, turtle soup, Oysters Rockefeller, lamb chops Bernaise and Café Brulot, producing a bill that, even though Galatoire's prices are very reasonable considering both the quality and the cachet, could have nonetheless underwritten a small European country.

Perhaps that marathon lunch was profligate, but I always wanted to feel like J.P. Morgan, John D. Rockefeller or any other self-respecting captain of American industry, and now I have.

Were I ever told that I would be allowed only one more New Orleans meal in my lifetime, I'd put on my seersucker suit and take my place in the legendary line that goes down Bourbon Street and often wraps around the corner. If you only have the opportunity for one memorable meal in "the city that care forgot," I recommend you do the same.

You'll find classic food, impeccable service and a room in which time can stand still if you make a point of ignoring the chiming of the clock. Just don't go looking for change, because they're fresh out.

Galatoire's
French Creole
209 Bourbon (between Iberville and Bienville Streets)
Lunch through dinner, Tuesday – Sunday
All major credit cards honored and
reservations may be made for upstairs and the steakhouse
Telephone: (504) 525-2021
Website: www.galatoires.com

Mandina's

*At some point in time, someone must have walked out of Mandina's looking for
more food—perhaps a sumo wrestler or a lumberjack coming off a three-day fast.*

The idea of opening a restaurant was the furthest thing from Sebastian
Mandina's mind.

It was 1898, the threshold of a new, twentieth century, and Mandina had emigrated from Palermo, Sicily, to New Orleans in order to
open a corner grocery in the growing Mid-City area. With his family
settled in upstairs, he opened his store and started chipping off his piece
of the American Dream.

Over time, the grocery evolved into a pool hall that sold sandwiches,
and the business was handed down to the two sons who continued to live
above the store. By 1932, the Great Depression had arrived, and Frank
and Anthony Mandina decided their financial future would be more se-
cure if it depended upon serving full meals to families instead of sandwiches to shooters and sharks. It was an idea that made sense for the times.

It still makes perfect sense today, as evidenced by the lines waiting
for tables in the same building on the corner of Canal and Cortez
Streets, where the same family (albeit several generations downstream)
dishes out their now time-honored Creole-Italian brand of New Orleans home cooking.

Mandina's has been self-described as "the quintessential New
Orleans neighborhood restaurant," and few would disagree. With its
pedigree including a grocery and a pool room, Mandina's makes no
pretense of being anything other than what it is: namely, a place that has
continually evolved into what New Orleanians want it to be instead of a

high-flying innovator hoping the city may follow its lead.

Beyond a modicum of kitchen modernizing and gussying up the bar and dining rooms after Hurricane Katrina poured several feet of water in the door, little has changed. The food is the same, the atmosphere is equally comfortable and the family went out of its way to make sure the faces throughout the operation remained the same.

Walking into Mandina's for the first or fiftieth time is an exercise in sudden comfort. The room and the bar area are nice enough, yet pleasantly informal. Large windows look through neon onto one of the quieter stretches of Canal Street, where red streetcars rumble by on a regular basis. Framed JazzFest posters adorn the walls, occasionally interspersed with old photographs. There are no booths, only tables and chairs. With its high ceilings, the room levels ambient noise into an even, yet lively buzz.

The room is a natural showcase of democracy having dinner. It is not uncommon to see a table of businessmen having a martini before lunch next to a table of blue-jeaned inhabitants from the surrounding neighborhoods to three generations of a family celebrating Grandma's birthday to a couple on a first date. The amount of people watching seems minimal, most people appearing absorbed in negotiating their way through exceedingly generous plates of food.

At some point in time, someone must have walked out of Mandina's looking for more food — perhaps a sumo wrestler or a lumberjack coming off a three-day fast. For mere mortals, however, most portions of most items are large enough to share. The rest are even bigger.

Consider starting with the onion rings. An "appetizer" portion is served on a platter that will easily feed four as a starter (and a "side" of French fries is even larger). The rings themselves show years of patron pleasing experience in the kitchen; they're thin enough not to be daunting, but not so thin that they droop or break the moment they're picked up. On a recent visit, our server was kind enough to ask The Sensible One and me if we'd like a half-order, something that doesn't appear on the menu or that we even knew existed. "No, go ahead and give us a regular order," we said. Foolishly.

I used to believe I always ordered Mandina's homemade turtle soup au sherry as a matter of habit until I realized the habit had grown into a ritual. Watch the soup arrive at the table. Wait for the server to ask if I'd like a little more sherry and wait for the bottle to be instantly produced. Say "please." Smile as the server adds somewhere between a dash and a dollop to give it some wallop. Dig in, knowing all is right in the world for the next few minutes, anyway.

Over the years, turtle soup has changed, much like New Orleans itself. Originally made from sea turtles weighing up to 1,000 pounds, ecological and conservation considerations have caused many turtle soup chefs to specify smaller, freshwater specimens, which numerous people believe have a gamier, brackish taste. This flavor is sometimes smoothed out through the addition or substitution of other meats, normally veal or pork, in the soup's preparation. In some instances, the substitution is terrapin, a smaller, East Coast turtle with a taste some epicures proclaim superior.

Turtle soup is a polarizing dish. It seems that no one greets it with indifference; they love it or loathe it. The soup appears on numerous menus throughout the city, but New Orleans partisans will almost always include Mandina's and one of the Brennan family outposts (usually Commander's Palace or Dickie Brennan's French Quarter steakhouse) among their top two or three favorites. For visitors unfamiliar with classic Crescent City preparations of turtle soup, Mandina's is a very good place to get a first taste.

For a city of big, wide-ranging appetites, Mandina's menu has expanded to fit them all. Steaks, chops, chicken, seafood, soups, salads, and sides join a variety of Italian, daily and house specials, along with a list of burgers, a muffuletta and poor boys that hearken back to the restaurant's earlier life as a pool hall.

While such a wide selection can be confusing, even intimidating, the real heart of Mandina's menu is to be found in its House Specials section, a half-dozen seafood entrees that are the foundation of the restaurant's venerable popularity. Among them are speckled trout, fresh catfish from legendary Bayou Des Allemands and seasonal soft shell crabs, all prepared in the classically simple New Orleans Meuniere or Almandine styles. But if there is one special that truly blends the city's Creole and Italian culinary cultures, it's the Gilled Shrimp over Pasta Bordelaise.

"Bordelaise" New Orleans style should not be confused with the Bordeaux district in France or the rich sauces laden with shallots and herbs that bear the same name. In New Orleans, Bordelaise can be translated to "garlic, butter, garlic, leaf parsley, garlic, occasional thyme and, oh yeah, garlic." The dish is the essence of simplicity itself. Plump, fresh Louisiana shrimp are grilled before being dumped atop a mountain of thin spaghetti drenched in this buttery, garlicky sauce. The portion size is enormous to the point The Sensible One and I normally split an order and still leave some on the platter. In the dish's sheer simplicity, every flavor comes through in an inspired blend. Yes, there's enough garlic that you'll want to take a roll of breath mints. Hell, you might think of taking two, but this is old style New Orleans Italian cooking at its best and most generous.

Mandina's is anything but tony, hip or au courant. It's a working class family restaurant that's been catering to local tastes instead of creating them for three-quarters of a century.

And boy, does it work.

One final note: Unless you show up a few minutes before the doors open or prefer to dine in the middle of the afternoon, you should expect to wait for a table, particularly on weekends. Reservations aren't accepted for parties of less than six, and credit cards have finally become accepted. Should you find this way of doing business particularly old-fashioned, you may want to tell a member of the family. He or she will no doubt thank you for it.

Mandina's Restaurant

Creole Italian

3800 Canal St (at South Cortez)

Lunch though dinner daily

Credit cards accepted

Reservations for less than six are not accepted

Telephone: 504-482-9179

Website: www.mandinasrestaurant.com

Mosca's

With Marcello's rising star came rising fortunes, and with them came one Provino Mosca, an Italian emigrant to Chicago who took little time in gathering both a criminal record and an irresistible item on his résumé: personal chef for Al Capone.

At the end of the old Western, The Man Who Shot Liberty Valance, a seasoned publisher tells a young buck reporter, "This is the West, sir. When the legend becomes fact, print the legend."

Whenever I hear the line, I think of Mosca's.

If New Orleans is anything, it is a decidedly Southern city. As a lot, Southerners embrace their ghosts, spin yarns about them and if the whole truth happens to get in the way, well, print the legend.

The first time I was taken to Mosca's, many years ago, I was thoroughly convinced I was about to be killed and eaten. It's in a nondescript, white plank roadhouse on a long, flat stretch of U.S. Highway 90 about five miles west of the Huey P. Long Bridge. In fact, at first glance, it's easy to mistake the place as abandoned. These days, there are more hints of civilization around it than there used to be, but that's not saying much.

If you arrive after sundown, you'll hear the steady drone of insects and the occasional mating call of frogs from the 178-acre parcel of swamp that runs along the south side of the highway and protects the roadhouse from both sides and the rear. Listen harder and you may start telling yourself you hear the ghosts of several dozen deadbeat gamblers, stool pigeons and double-crossing goombahs, all reputedly wrapped in chains and dispatched to eternity in the slime beneath the marshland's boggy waters.

If anyone knows the whole story about Mosca's, they're not talking, no doubt a wise choice. There's a history section on the restaurant's website, and it tells the story of hard-working, patriotic Italian immigrants who, with grit, gumption, elbow grease and pluck, claimed their modest patch of the American Dream along a forlorn highway. It's a great story, as far as it goes, but the legends surrounding Mosca's suggest it doesn't go far enough.

In its earliest years, the nondescript building was known as the Willswood Tavern, which looked more or less like any roadside bar in any south Louisiana parish. The tavern had once been an abandoned shed on the acreage that was owned by the Marcello family, alleged to have deep Mafia connections. At the end of World War II, Carlos Marcello (1910-1993), known behind his back as "The Little Man," came to be regarded as "boss" of all organized crime operations in New Orleans, and Sundays at the Willswood became legendary.

From Lake Charles in the west to Gulfport (Mississippi) in the east, family captains and lieutenants would make their way to the don's unofficial headquarters at the Willswood to pay tribute (as well as his "taste" of the take) to Marcello. Throughout the morning and into the afternoon, a steady procession of bookies, madams, fences, corrupt law enforcement officials, greased-palm politicos, loan sharks and other "associates" would take care of business with il padrone. Once the serious work was done, rivers of wine would flow, plate upon plate of Italian food would stream out of the kitchen and the raucous party would continue until the shadows grew long and daylight drew short.

With Marcello's rising star came rising fortunes, and with them came one Provino Mosca, an Italian emigrant to Chicago who took little time in gathering both a criminal record and an irresistible item on his résumé: personal chef for Al Capone. Marcello installed Mosca in the kitchen of the Willswood and even went so far as to build a house for the chef's family close to the tavern.

Circa 1960, Marcello moved his headquarters from the Willswood and the restaurant, already growing famous, became Mosca's. Part of the legend is that Marcello gifted both the restaurant and its surrounding acreage of swamp to the Mosca family. Maybe that's true, and maybe it isn't, but either way, it makes a charming asterisk, so print the legend.

Provino Mosca passed on in 1962, followed by Carlos Marcello in 1993. Over the ensuing years, the restaurant has come to more closely resemble what is written in the website's antiseptic history than the embodiment of a dark and sinister world, which would rightly include black sedans with rolled steel mudguards, the chatter of Thompson submachine guns, whispering godfathers, Mustache Petes, wise guys, goombahs and gun molls. No matter how colorful such imagery may be, the real legend is considerably more flavorful.

More than sixty years after Provino Mosca first walked into the roadhouse kitchen, successive generations of his family continue to put out some of New Orleans' best Sicilian-by-way-of-the-bayou cooking, cucina that earned the restaurant designation as one of "America's Classics" in the 1998 James Beard Awards. In a city where you rarely have to venture more than a few blocks to find superlative food, crowds of local residents continue to trek desolate miles to pack the place.

The menu is surprisingly short. Only four specialties are listed along with four types of spaghetti, a filet mignon, quail, Cornish hen and a homemade sausage that could very well be the city's gold standard.

The four specialties are worth special note. Least famous among the four is a traditional chicken cacciatore, which allows diners to evaluate the kitchen's comparative chops, considering the ubiquity of the dish in America's Italian restaurants. In the same neighborhood is Chicken à la Grande, the house variation on classic rosemary chicken, but amped up with generous amounts of olive oil, white wine and enough garlic to send Dracula scurrying back to Transylvania. Somewhat sheepishly, I confess to avoiding the à la Grande on my first visits to Mosca's, mistakenly thinking it would prove a rather pedestrian chicken dish. After one bite, I stood corrected.

The two specialties that attract the most attention are the eponymous Shrimp and Oysters Mosca. Shrimp Mosca is an Italianized adaptation of traditional New Orleans-style barbecue shrimp — sautéed in plenty of butter with torqued-up garlic, rosemary and oregano. Despite the similarity in names, the Oysters Mosca are confidently seasoned, topped with a hearty layer of breadcrumbs and baked in an old-fashioned metal pie pan. Both dishes are, in a word, peerless.

Despite the brevity of the menu, it remains a test of indecision. Repeat customers have learned the only workable formula to remedy their wavering is to bring as many people as they can pack in their car, have everyone order something different, put it all in the center of the table and go after it "family style." The only drawback I've found to this system is that while I get a taste of everything, I never seem to get enough of anything.

Time doesn't have much meaning at Mosca's. Everything is cooked to order, and some dishes take close to an hour to get to the table. This sometimes leads to the staggered delivery of plates, and if all the plates happen to reach your party at the same time, don't be overly surprised if the temperatures prove inconsistent. The only known cure for this situation is another glass of wine. Cent'anni!

A couple of caveats are in order. First, they don't take reservations on Saturday night except for very large parties. Even though the restaurant accepts reservations Tuesday through Friday nights, expect a wait, sometimes quite lengthy. Secondly, like many old-line New Orleans restaurants, the only coin of the realm honored is cash.

Finally, in terms of ambiance, Mosca's remains an unadorned roadhouse after sixty-plus years, and several generations of New Orleanians wouldn't have it any other way. A nibble here, a nibble there and neither will you.

Mosca's Restaurant
Creole Italian
4137 U.S. Highway 90 West, Avondale
Dinner, Tuesday - Saturday
Cash only
Reservations accepted
Call (504) 436–8950 or 504-436–9942
after 4:30 p.m. to make reservations
Website: www.moscasrestaurant.com

The Bon Ton Café

A fuzzy line separates the traditional from the trendy when it comes to New Orleans restaurants, a line across which the Bon Ton refuses to stray.

Don't let the checkered tablecloths fool you.

They're nothing more than a clever disguise in a Central Business District restaurant where the food is so good you'd swear it was being served on white linen by tuxedoed waiters and overseen by a persnickety French martinet in the kitchen.

In actuality, however, almost everything about The Bon Ton Café is the antithesis of what most people would immediately associate if someone said "French restaurant," everything, that is, except the bravura of the kitchen.

Perhaps the most startling thing about the Bon Ton is the fact that, despite its premier location smack in the middle of downtown New Orleans, it is generally overlooked by lifelong residents and for all practical purposes unknown by visitors. When I mention the Bon Ton to my Crescent City neighbors, the most common response is, "Gosh, I haven't been there for years." A recommendation to friends visiting the city is invariably met with a blank stare.

While such a lack of recognition would seem to be a surefire recipe for any restaurant's failure, the Bon Ton is busy enough to be any owner's dream. It is only open for lunch and dinner on weekdays. It doesn't take reservations at lunch, and if you're not there by quarter until noon, you might as well hang it up and look elsewhere. Trying to get in for dinner without a reservation falls somewhere between overoptimistic and harebrained. Weekends are reserved for private parties, providing the guest list is long enough, and the host's bank account is commensurately flush.

One of the clichés I grew to loathe during my misspent advertising stretch was, "We advertise on our plate," usually the transparent cop-out of a cheapskate trying to pass himself off as the canny proprietor of an upscale establishment. In that respect, The Bon Ton Café is one of the few places where I've been forced to eat my words along with a substantial helping of crow.

In the forty or so years that New Orleans has served as first a weekend getaway and then a home, never have I seen any sort of advertising for the Bon Ton beyond a sporadic listing in a magazine's directory section, and rarely have I seen that. Like the lack of need to maintain regular weekend hours, it is apparent that the Bon Ton also sees no real reason to advertise. And while such a combination is uncommon in this day of relentless marketing hyperbole, there is a fundamental rightness to it that befits the Bon Ton in the same, somewhat old-fashioned way the Bon Ton reflects the classic dining heritage that is fading from the city's restaurant industry.

A fuzzy line separates the traditional from the trendy when it comes to New Orleans restaurants, a line across which the Bon Ton refuses to stray. And yet somehow in so doing, the restaurant has blossomed into an heirloom instead of withering into an anachronism.

No one seems to be able to pin down an exact opening date for the Bon Ton. The best guess is the early 1900s, when the restaurant opened as yet another Creole establishment. In the early 1950s, the fading Creole eatery was taken over and reinvented by Al and Alzona Pierce, who infused the menu with the more rustic Cajun cooking of their native Lafourche and Terrebonne parishes.

To New Orleanians who had made their way to the city from the less urbane parishes of Southwest Louisiana, the Bon Ton provided a welcomed "taste of home." The earthier Cajun cuisine soon found its own following among born-and-bred city dwellers with their more classically refined Creole palates.

For more than twenty years, the Bon Ton remained one of the

few upscale Cajun restaurants on the Crescent City's culinary landscape, until a kid from Opelousas came along. The kid was Paul Prudhomme, brought back home to Louisiana by the Brennan family as executive chef at Commander's Palace. Playful by nature and innovative by intuition, Prudhomme combined the earthiness of Cajun cooking and the more urbane traditions of Creole cuisine into the hybrid style that ultimately became known and accepted as Louisiana fusion.

Prudhomme left Commander's and went on to refine his self-invented Blackened Redfish in his own restaurant, K-Paul's Louisiana Kitchen, before ultimately emerging as New Orleans' first culinary superstar of the modern era. Meanwhile, a second generation of the Pierce family assumed the helm of the Bon Ton and chose to remain true to the restaurant's Cajun roots.

The differences between K-Paul's hybrid tinkering and the Bon Ton's adherence to its Cajun heritage are noticeable and striking, but there is one dish coming out of each kitchen where the similarities are so marked it begs the question: Which restaurant cooked it up first?

That dish is Crawfish Étouffée, the rich, redolent and roux-based stew that derives its name from the French word for "smothered." Despite its French-ified name, crawfish étouffée is generally regarded as a mainstay of Cajun cuisine, where the roux (a mixture of flour simmered in oil or rendered fat) used as both a flavoring and binding agent is traditionally cooked until reaching a brown so deep its color borders on that of black coffee. The roux is used to cook the "trinity" (celery, onion and bell pepper), spices and seafood stock are blended in before the dish is finished with crawfish tails and served around mounded rice.

In the more citified Creole cooking, flour is blended into an oil and fat (often butter) but the finished roux is normally lighter in color. It can end up being the basis for a broad number of sauces, from the snowy Bechamel to one as medium-to-dark brown as the classic marchand du vin.

Rather than the dark Cajun sauce with its dense, smoky flavors or its lighter Creole cousin, the roux that's the basis for the crawfish étouffée served at both Bon Ton and K-Paul's is coppery red, a color that requires a quick eye and a steady hand to produce. This is especially true in commercial restaurants where roux prepared to order is often cooked over blazing temperatures causing the color to dramatically change in a matter of seconds.

The result of the reddish roux is a dish where the flavors of the crawfish and spices rise above their sauce instead of being overpowered by its smoky density. At K-Paul's the final product may be spectacular, but somehow at The Bon Ton Café the experience reaches heights bordering on the transcendental. At a lunch during the apex of the spring crawfish season, my former client and longtime pal Banker Bill took one bite and proclaimed it "Perfect." When I agreed with him that it was first-rate, Bill looked across the table to me and said, "No, perfect."

While modern aquaculture techniques and deceptively marketed Chinese imports now make it possible for New Orleans restaurants to serve crawfish on a year-'round basis, true Louisiana crawfish flourishes in a limited season running from Mardi Gras to early June, with the prime months being April and May. The extended availability allows the Bon Ton to offer a variety of crawfish dishes throughout the year, but prime time is prime time so plan to get them while they're at the pinnacle.

If you can't, don't despair. Some type of seafood is always in season in South Louisiana and you'd better believe the Bon Ton hasn't stayed in business for a century-plus by trying to pass off second-tier seafood to food-crazy residents in one of America's culinary capitals. While it's true that the widest variety of seafood is at its peak from spring into summer, the kitchen at the Bon Ton has demonstrated an almost preternatural ability to find the freshest seafood available, prepare it with finesse and deliver it to your checkered tablecloth.

Pan broiled Gulf shrimp in a lemon garlic sauce. Salty, sweet oysters. Native speckled trout. Soft-shell crabs. Turtle soup. Redfish caught off Louisiana's Golden Meadows fishing grounds. Crabmeat Imperial or au gratin. At dinner, they even offer steaks and veal, although for the life of me, I can't figure out why. Seafood is the raison d'etre for The Bon Ton Café, and unless you suffer from an unfortunate allergy, plant a period on it.

In contrast to the elegant seafood coming out of the kitchen, the dining room at the Bon Ton is unpretentious with its brick wall, windows looking onto historic Natchez and Magazine Streets, four wrought-iron chandeliers and tablecloths that would seem to be more at home in a cozy Italian trattoria. The servers, several of whom have been there several years longer than forever, are relaxed in a home-style way. Nonetheless, I recommend that a gent wear a jacket so he may be mistaken for some of the lawyers, bankers, and business leaders, particularly during lunch. If you don't, no one will say a word, but this is old-school New Orleans, where visitors may be greeted like welcome guests, but regular customers are treated like gods.

In its circa 1840 building in the heart of downtown New Orleans, The Bon Ton Café is one of the last outposts of the historic, gracious city that has survived hurricanes, floods, Huey Long, football fans reduced to wearing grocery sacks on their heads, countless generations of Mardi Gras and later laughed about all of it over an unapologetically lazy lunch. Those of us who cherish the grace of this remarkable city can only pray the Bon Ton's hourglass never runs low on sand.

The Bon Ton Café
Cajun seafood
401 Magazine Street (at Natchez St.)
Lunch and dinner, Monday - Friday
Credit cards accepted
Reservations accepted for dinner
Telephone: 504-524-3386
Website: http://www.thebontoncafe.com

Casamento's

A typical dozen will usually contain both smaller oysters with their intense flavor and some so large you'll suspect that if they ever produced pearls, they'd be large enough to play golf with.

The difference between two of New Orleans' most venerated and revered oyster bars can be summarized in one simple sentence:

Casamento's is for purists, and the Acme is for tourists.

While such a statement may seem uncomplimentary at face value, it is not a knock on the food served at either establishment, since most New Orleanians would put both places in the city's top five classic oyster bars.

The differences between the two can be found in the addresses and attitudes toward change. The Acme is located in the tourist end of the upper French Quarter, between Bourbon and Royal Streets, while Casamento's can be found near the corner of Napoleon and Magazine in a more genteel residential and shopping district.

In the last fifteen years, Acme has opened four new satellite locations, including one in Destin (Florida), while Casamento's has stayed in the twenty-foot wide storefront where they opened their doors in 1919.

When sushi was all the rage in the early 1990s, Acme tossed some scallions and wasabi on their raw oysters and touted them as "Cajun Sushi." When another New Orleans restaurant, Drago's, developed the charbroiled oysters that took the city by storm, "chargrilled oysters" quickly appeared on the Acme menu. By contrast, Casamento's has stuck with the oyster basics — on the half shell, fried and oyster stew — and watched the fads pass by their doorstep. In fact, it was only in 2012 that

Casamento's broke down and started serving its own version of char-broiled oysters in the evening.

Whether Casamento's dogged resistance to change has been created by over 90 years of success or plain old hardheadedness on the part of the owners is difficult to say, but the bottom line is, it works for them.

On the history page of the restaurant's website is a photograph of the front room taken in 1919. With the exception of the tiles on the counter front, a few different pictures on the walls and some updated equipment, it is nearly identical to the view you get when you first walk in the door. That sameness extends into the second dining room as well.

While there's no way of knowing if Italian immigrant Joe Casamento could envision a ninety-six year run for his restaurant, one of his key early decisions has made it possible for the place to make very few changes as the decades have danced by. Following restaurant traditions of his native Italy, Casamento had tiles installed on all the floors and walls to make the restaurant easy to clean. In fact, so many tiles were ordered for the restaurant's initial installation that it took four separate tile companies from across the United States to fill the order.

This selfsame order of tile still covers the floor and lower ten feet of walls today, and the place remains spotless. Original tile also surrounds the twin picture windows, front door, and transoms, giving Casamento's storefront façade its frozen-in-time quality.

While such timeless visual elements enhance both Casamento's aesthetics and charm, it's not the architecture or décor that's served on the plate. It's the food in general and the oysters in particular.

Should you arrive for an early lunch before the doors open at eleven, the chances are fairly good that you'll be met with the reassuring sight of men with burlap bags on their shoulders delivering the day's freshly caught oysters. If you're seated in the front room and take the opportunity to watch the speed and sure-handedness with which the shuckers work, you'll realize that not only did you arrive for lunch before your lunch ever showed up, but the whole process happened in a number of minutes you can count on your fingers.

It is at this point where visitors from outside the Gulf of Mexico's main oystering centers (running from Abbeville, Louisiana, to Apalachicola, Florida) come face to face with a conflict raging between coastal seafood harvesters and overreaching federal bureaucrats hell-bent on creating a "nanny state." At the center of the controversy is if and to what degree eating raw oysters can be potentially dangerous to human health.

For nearly twenty years, a disclaimer has appeared on menus in most oyster bars warning of health hazards associated with eating raw shellfish. The reason for the somewhat disconcerting warning is Vibrio vulnificus, a bacterium that naturally occurs in some oysters. While nothing in this essay should be construed as a professional medical opinion (yes, we writers have to put down disclaimers, too), a combination of facts, history and common sense suggests that the vast majority of the populace have little to nothing to fear from consuming raw oysters.

The truth is, people with serious pre-existing health conditions, such as liver disease, cancer, diabetes, AIDS or other autoimmunity problems, account for virtually all illnesses and deaths (about fifteen per year nationwide) from raw oyster consumption. Actuarial figures suggest that a person is far more likely to die from a lightning strike than seafood consumption. Nonetheless, people with conditions putting them at risk are advised to only eat oysters that have been cooked, frozen or pasteurized — a recommendation that already appears on many oyster bar menus. (In fact, Casamento's menu contains: "Warning: There may be a risk associated with consuming raw shellfish as is the case with other raw protein products. If you suffer from chronic illness of the liver, stomach, or blood, or have other immune disorders, you should eat these products fully cooked.")

That said, the oysters on the half shell at Casamento's are magnificent. A typical dozen will usually contain both smaller oysters with their intense flavor and some so large you'll suspect that if they ever produced pearls, they'd be large enough to play golf with.

Fried oysters and shrimp are available as dinners or as "boats," which are not traditional New Orleans poor boys, but overflowing sandwiches made with the equivalent of Texas toast. Catfish, trout, and seasonal soft-shell crabs are also available in both configurations.

The pocket-sized kitchen also produces chicken tenders, spaghetti and meatballs and a seafood combo platter, while a gumbo pot simmers and their overworked fryers produce a steady stream of crab claw and calamari plates.

While there is any number of places to grab a great dozen or two on the half shell in New Orleans, there is an old-fashioned, turn-back-the-clock quality about Casamento's that separates it from the pack. Perhaps the restaurant being closed every June, July and August best illustrates this. Years ago, oysters were traditionally served only in months with an "R" in their spellings. While it's true that summer months remain less than optimal for mollusk harvesting, improved oystering techniques have made the "R" rule more of a myth than anything else. That doesn't mean you won't see some plaque reading, "Oysters 'R' in Season" in oyster bars all across America, although I've never noticed one in Casamento's.

Even though the restaurant stays open through part of the "R-less" month of May, there remains a charm to its contrarian adherence to myth. And it's that devotion to times past which makes Casamento's the Crescent City's quintessential oyster house, at least for purists.

Casamento's Restaurant
Oysters
4330 Magazine St. (at Napoleon)
Lunch, Tuesday - Saturday
Dinner, Thursday - Saturday
Closed June, July and August
Cash only and no reservations
Telephone: (504) 895-9761
Website: www.casamentosrestaurant.com

Willie Mae's Scotch House

Ten years ago, the place was an insider's secret — a neighborhood place in a dangerous neighborhood, dishing up plates of fried chicken with no suspicion it was on the threshold of becoming a culinary legend in one of America's great dining cities.

Willie Mae's Scotch House started life as a corner tavern in 1957 in one half of a double shotgun house on a dicey street corner in the Fauborg Tremé section of New Orleans, the oldest African American suburb in the United States and one where urban re-gentrification has started to gain a game-changing foothold in the wake of Katrina.

Somewhere along the line, proprietor Willie Mae Seaton started frying chicken for the saloon's customers. And, boy oh boy, could Willie Mae cook.

As the decades meandered by, word slowly got around about what Willie Mae was plucking out of her cast iron skillets and deep fat fryer. Oh, sure there was a pork chop, a veal cutlet and the occasional seafood dish, but the people were coming for the chicken, with most of them choosing the place's creamy red beans and rice on the side.

Then came March 2005.

In the annual James Bead Foundation Awards, the most prestigious industry citations in the country, Willie Mae's Scotch House was named one of America's Classics, a special designation for outstanding regional restaurants and cuisine. Traveling foodies from across the nation started including Willie Mae's on epicurean pilgrimages to the corner of St. Ann and Tonti in the Crescent City. Lines got long, then longer. The cash box filled up quicker. After 48 years, the place was an overnight success.

A short five months later came August 29. Katrina. The storm.

The bitch. The collapsing levee system and water that wouldn't stop until eighty percent of one of America's most storied cities was underwater. The red, spray-painted hieroglyphics on doors and walls telling of horrors lying within. The stench of forsaken death on 95-degree afternoons in a powerless city.

Willie Mae's Scotch House was not spared. Her restaurant and connected home were flooded, and Willie Mae Seaton herself was nearly ninety years old. The very notion of starting over was more than her tired bones could bear. But in a city where food grows from a topic of conversation into a hobby and finally into an obsession, the idea of life without Willie Mae's golden fried yardwalker was unbearable to the municipal belly.

What happened next bespeaks volumes about the kindness of Deep South strangers. With the spirit of an Amish country barn raising, people united only by appetites for good food and good works rolled up their sleeves, picked up often-unfamiliar tools and pitched in. Spearheaded by the Southern Foodways Alliance, a ragtag coalition of writers, chefs and everyday chowhounds dedicated to protecting the culinary traditions of the American South, an army of volunteers spent more than a year of weekends repairing and restoring the Scotch House.

Willie Mae's Scotch House reopened under the watchful eye of Willie Mae and in the more than capable hands of her great-granddaughter Kerry, the only person to whom the kitchen's secrets have ever been entrusted.

While the James Beard Award had made the restaurant famous to a small, passionate band of foodophiles, designation by Food Network as the best place for fried chicken in America, along with regular mentions from media über-chefs John Besh and Emeril Lagasse among others, put Willie Mae's in the middle of the media mainstream.

Business is booming these days at the Scotch House. Steady streams of taxis disgorge French Quarter tourists and convention delegates at the front door, and the waits are getting longer at the no reservations, two-room restaurant. Grumblings from locals that "their" place was being overrun with outsiders were inevitable.

The Sensible One and I have made about a half-dozen visits since Katrina. Has the fried chicken continue to live up to its pre-ballyhoo reputation? It has. The red beans remain as good as any I've had anywhere, and the home-squeezed lemonade makes for a remarkably refreshing washdown. The tab runs slightly over thirty dollars including tax and a nice, but not extravagant tip for the pleasant young gentlemen who serve us.

We have had absolutely no complaint about anything.

But these days, I'm getting scared.

While sudden success may not have killed off as many restaurants as chronic under-capitalization, it's taken out more than its fair share. Try as hard as I might to look the other way, I'm beginning to see the telltale signals of a place that has its eyes on expansion and possibly not keeping an eye on what they already have.

Business hours are expanding. Willie Mae's remains a lunch-only place but posted hours have expanded from ten until five Monday through Saturday.

They've started to serve beer. Despite Scotch House's origins as a tavern, the place had been dry for years. While anyone who knows me might find my objection to an eatery selling beer ironic if not downright comical, there has always been a certain charm to be found in a cafe that actually makes all its money selling food. Also, a restaurateur's knowledge that he or she will succeed or fail based totally upon the quality of the food will make for a restaurateur who keeps a sharper eye on the quality of what's coming out of the kitchen.

In a nod to the realities of today's America, Willie Mae's has started accepting all major credit cards. For years, the cash only status and lack of an on-premises ATM offered the amusing moment of a panicked out-of-town customer trying to choose between finding a cash machine in a dicey part of the city or facing the grim prospect of a long afternoon washing chicken grease off dishes in a crowded scullery.

I had spent great amounts of time in New Orleans over the course of thirty years without ever hearing about Willie Mae's Scotch House. Now it's in nearly every tourism publication in the city with ads pushing the Food Network "Best Chicken" designation and other televised kudos.

Uh-oh.

It's unsporting at best to chastise restaurateurs for capitalizing on glittering reviews that start bringing in so many customers that expansion becomes inevitable. But I can think of few prospects more deplorable than Willie Mae's Scotch House opening a new location seating 200 somewhere along a soulless commercial strip in a suburb like Kenner or Marrero, the kind of place where a twenty-foot tall neon drumstick would fit right in.

As it turns out, Willie Mae's started expanding in 2014 with one new location and a second on the way. I'm old-fashioned and ornery enough to ignore the new locations, preferring love-powered originals to profit-driven "equivalents."

I don't pretend to be smart enough to tell anyone the secret of the success Willie Mae's Scotch House is currently enjoying. My suspicion is that it's a combination of its very limited menu, dining rooms that aren't too big for its small kitchen and a dogged determination to make sure that everything is not only cooked to order, but cooked the way Willie Mae herself would were she still manning the skillets.

All too often, the price of changing success is failure. A key question is whether or not the new generation, personified by great-granddaughter Kerry Seaton, will have the patience to continue doing the same old thing in the same old way that made a small fried chicken joint in Tremé an American culinary landmark. All of us can only hope she will.

Within the time remaining before she has to make her decision, go there.

Since the above was first written, I've had a chance to keep looking in on Willie Mae's with two of my "running buddies": Slider Bob and The Marlboro Man. After one of those visits, I updated my thoughts. Some of them may prove redundant and, for that, I ask your forbearance.

It was more a matter of luck than good planning when I found my old pal "Slider" Bob on the other end of the ringing telephone, asking me the name of the fried chicken place I'm always raving about.

Slider had a delivery to make across the Mississippi River on Algiers Point, and rather than give him directions, it was easier to ask if he had an empty passenger seat. All he had to say was that he did, and that was that. It was a cloudless morning with a hint of spring in it and the lure of lunch at Willie Mae's was far more compelling than the prospect of a day wrangling nouns and verbs in advance of a looming deadline.

To understand the appeal of such a slothful day, you should understand a little about Slider and a lot about Willie Mae's.

I can think of no better advertisement for reincarnation than the possibility of coming back for another lifetime go-round as Slider Bob. He's bald, middle-aged, undemanding and equally unassuming. He loves good food, finds it everywhere he happens to be, yet has shown the iron will to give up enough of it to lose sixty pounds without cutting a single drop from his prodigious consumption of beer.

New Orleans has always been a fried chicken town (the Popeye's chain was founded here, for heaven's sake), and any discussion of whose is best can serve as the preamble to a protracted argument. Every place that fries chicken wants to put their name into the discussion, of course, but among the places most often mentioned are Dooky Chase's, Fiorella's in the French Quarter, Lil' Dizzy's on Esplanade and, of course, Willie Mae's Scotch House.

It seems that every New Orleans restaurant has both a "secret ingredient" and a determination to never reveal it, and Willie Mae's is no exception. If you buy into the legend (and why not?), you'll discover that Willie Mae passed down her closely guarded secret only to her great-granddaughter, Kerry, who runs the restaurant to this day. In a National Public Radio interview, Kerry let it slip that the secret was using a "wet batter" and salt and pepper as the only spices. This was all well and good until people started trying to duplicate the recipe at home with predictably unsuccessful results.

Had the Scotch House been located somewhere other than Tremé, there's little doubt that fame would have come quicker. New Orleans can be a very odd town, in more ways than those that are obvious.

While talking about places to eat is seemingly the city's favorite sport (even more so than their beloved Saints), a lot of people have a tendency to clam up when asked about their favorite restaurant, particularly when said place isn't conventional. It's as if talking about a place will cause it to suddenly fall prey to the curse of mediocrity.

Aided by this seeming conspiracy of silence among the locals, buzz about Willie Mae's fried chicken spread at a speed that could politely be called "glacial," but spread it did, especially when Willie Mae's Scotch House won its James Beard Award. That accolade even caught the attention of Slider, who began hinting that a road trip to a chicken joint sounded like a more than acceptable adventure (provided, of course, there would be plenty of beer).

Slider and I pulled up to the non-descript, white plank building that houses Willie Mae's at about 1:30 on a weekday when business in the not-too-distant French Quarter was lighter than usual. Roughly a dozen diners were milling in front of the plain white door. Occasionally, the front door would open and a group of two or four diners would jostle its way through those of us clustered on the sidewalk. Invariably one of them would tell us it was worth the wait.

The doorway at Willie Mae's is interesting in and of itself since, instead of a host taking names or a formal waiting line, it runs on an ersatz honor system. Essentially, once you no longer see anyone who was there when you arrived, it's your turn. By the time Slider and I were deemed to be the next through the doorway, the cluster had once again grown to a dozen or so diners, one of whom was a middle-aged woman seemingly undone by the relative informality of the situation. When she inquired as to the whereabouts of the line, she was told she was indeed in it. Commenting that it didn't seem very organized, she was advised that (a) she was in New Orleans, and (b) for New Orleans, this was a very organized line.

Finally, Slider and I were ushered into the sanctum sanctorum, a dining room with ten tables. The room is plain. The walls are white and covered mostly with posters and photos, the most recent addition of which seems to be of President Obama. The functional, institutional furniture is more practical than pricey. The overall look is what one might expect of a neighborhood soul food place. About the only thing out of place is the framed James Beard citation inconspicuously hanging beside the front door.

The menu is simple. It's fried chicken and a half-dozen sides. There are some other entrees listed, the reason why I don't know, since I've never seen anything but plates and platters of chicken make their way out the kitchen door. What's the point? This same kitchen door "research" indicated that the majority of customers picked red beans and rice as their side order. Slider fell into his "when in Rome" mindset and ordered the chicken and red beans; I've never ordered anything else at Willie Mae's and saw no reason to end a perfectly good streak.

The food at Willie Mae's is reputed to be cooked to order. Maybe it is, maybe not. Since at least ninety percent of the people coming in are ordering chicken and beans, I think it's far more likely that there are jumbo pots of beans and rice simmering on a back burner, and that chicken is being battered and dropped into hot oil as long as people are parading through the front door. Such idle speculations may be neither here nor there, since the food keeps coming out of the postage stamp of a kitchen at such a clip there isn't time or space for it to be anything but hot and fresh.

Once ordered, the wait for our food was between ten and fifteen minutes, during which time Slider Bob kept me entertained by constantly swiveling his head in expectation as a stream of plates paraded from the kitchen to other tables than ours. Our platter of chicken and plates of beans had no more hit the table when Slider grabbed a wing, trisected it and bit into the middle section.

Before the first droplet of Crystal hot sauce could land on my red beans, Slider had broken into a seraphic smile and, as I lip-synched along with him, I wondered how many thousands of people over the years had also rhapsodically claimed, "This is the best fried chicken I've ever had in my life."

Is the fried chicken at Willie Mae's Scotch House indeed the "best fried chicken in America," as it has been cited on Food Network and at least suggested by the James Beard Award? I make no pretense to be an arbiter of such matters, but I can think of none better in my half century of experience, nor have I ever heard anyone walking out of Willie Mae's claim "the chicken is better at (fill-in-the-blank)." It's crisp outside, moist inside and has a taste that, while essentially unadorned, is anything but bland.

Slider and I didn't talk much as we made short work of the chicken and beans, at least until there was a single breast forlornly sitting on the platter. I split it with a knife, but much to my surprise, Slider declined to take half, sighing "If I'd known it was going to really be this good, I would have ordered a side green salad instead of the beans." With each bite I subsequently took, he somehow managed to look even more crestfallen.

Not long ago, I was reading a blog in which someone gushed that Willie Mae's should be franchised into a national chain. I'm sure the softheaded son-of-a-bitch meant it as some sort of compliment, but the factors that make Willie Mae's such a success are anathema to such shallow enthusiasm. Despite the 2014 forays into new locations, the original place works because, by the numbers: it's ten tables small, open only 36 hours a week, defies the number one fundamental of real estate (location, location, location) and focuses 99% of its effort on preparing one item better than any other restaurant in America. And according to my old pal Slider Bob, "that puts 'em one up on any other chicken joint in the whole U.S. of A."

All I can add to that is a rousing "Amen."

Willie Mae's Scotch House
Soul Food, Fried Chicken
2401 St. Ann (on the corner of Tonti Street)
Lunch, Monday – Saturday
Accepts major credit cards, no reservations
Telephone: (504) 822-9503
No website

Every year some publication or another, not to mention any number of blog sites, will post a list of the city's best chefs. Sometimes it's a traditional "top ten," although I've seen longer and shorter lists.

What they all have in common, of course, is subjectivity, and the following list is no exception. In assembling the list of the four restaurants that follows, several factors have been taken into account.

In keeping with this guidebook's mission of focusing in upon restaurants where the fare leans more toward time-honored, traditional New Orleans offerings and preparations, chefs have been selected with an eye on those whose kitchens are as deeply rooted in Louisiana's food heritage than trailblazing innovations or current trends.

That's not to say that these remarkable chefs are doggedly adhering to century-old recipes or aren't open to advances that have occurred in the industry as both technologies and techniques have evolved over the years. Instead, they have focused their energies on presenting fresh, locally produced ingredients and harnessed their creativity in a way where their foodstuffs become enhanced rather than overpowered by eccentricity.

Case in point: the first chef, Paul Prudhomme, generally acknowledged as the reigning godfather of New Orleans headliners, successfully blended disparate elements of rustic Cajun cooking and the more citified Creole cuisine into a successful hybrid that has become the bedrock principle for an entire generation of successful Louisiana chefs.

Susan Spicer incorporates her predilection for more international flavors into Louisiana basics to produce her playful New World cuisine. Frank Brigtsen worked his way up through Prudhomme's flagship kitchen, the influences of which are still prominent in the dishes that have been coming out of his kitchen for twenty-five years. Donald Link learned many of his techniques as a sous chef for Spicer before opening his mini-chain of three-and-a-half New Orleans restaurants.

All four have learned that if they keep their focus on the food coming out of their kitchens, their reputations will take care of themselves.

In assembling a list limited by space, some people are going to get overlooked. In a somewhat arbitrary decision, both television celebrity chefs Emeril Lagasse and John Besh were bypassed because the commitments ensuing from their broadcast careers and numbers of successful restaurants are limiting the amounts of time either can spend in the kitchen. There are other up-and-coming chefs who are certainly nipping at the heels of their elders and find a legion of rising, even younger chefs nipping at theirs.

Disclaimers aside, here are four restaurants where, under the watchful eyes of four truly special chefs, the best of New Orleans' culinary traditions remain cherished yet changes come and, like the wheels of justice, grind slow but fine.

K-Paul's Louisiana Kitchen

The dish was christened "blackened" redfish, and it catapulted Paul Prudhomme into the national culinary spotlight, a place that seemed as comfortable to the man from Opelousas as a bayou is to a gator.

When a long line forms outside a New Orleans restaurant, it can often prove amusing to observe the reactions of some city residents. Should they know someone in line, they cite it as proof that New Orleans is one big street party where the locals sure know their food. Should they not, the restaurant is pilloried as a tourist place unworthy of local patronage.

For more than fifteen years, Paul Prudhomme saw plenty of the latter at the front door of K-Paul's, his runaway success of a restaurant in the French Quarter. When opened in 1979, the restaurant had a miniscule capacity of 62 guests, creating the need for "community seating," the polite euphemism for guests from more than one party being required to share a table with others. The arrangement was tolerated when K-Paul's was only open at lunch, but when the restaurant expanded its operation to serve dinner, people started to balk at the notion of sharing a relatively pricey dinner with total strangers.

People grumbled and griped about seating and other rules instituted to keep things manageable for the small restaurant, but they kept flocking to K-Paul's because a revolution was taking place in Prudhomme's tiny kitchen.

For generations, diners in New Orleans had been hardwired into Creole cuisine, the refined style of cooking cobbled together from the foods of many nations, but with its underpinnings being predominantly French. The other Louisiana niche cuisine was Cajun, a heartier country style of cooking from Bayou Country, commonly dismissed as rustic by city dwellers. In fact, when Prudhomme opened K-Paul's in 1979, there was only one authentic Cajun "A-list" restaurant of any real renown in New Orleans, the Bon Ton Café with roots going back to the early 1900s.

Prudhomme, the caboose of thirteen children from a Cajun farming family in Opelousas, spent a great part of his childhood cooking with his mother to feed the rest of the family, which worked the fields. He opened and closed a pair of restaurants before he was thirty and worked in kitchens across America before landing a job, at age 35, as the executive chef at Commander's Palace, which had just been taken over by the Brennans, New Orleans' family of celebrated restaurateurs.

It was at Commander's where Prudhomme's star shot skyward. By integrating Cajun ingredients and techniques into the Creole cuisine upon which the restaurant had built its reputation, Prudhomme created the new fusion cuisine that came to be generally known as "Louisiana" or "South Louisiana" cooking. While at Commander's, Prudhomme revised classic New Orleans recipes for the Brennans, including barbecue shrimp, turtle soup and others, a number of which are still served today in the family's various restaurants.

If Prudhomme's star was rising at Commander's, it was at K-Paul's where it went stratospheric, and it was primarily due to a remarkably simple idea that blended nine everyday herbs and spices, some butter and a piece of local fish in a black iron skillet so hot it literally smoked. The dish was christened "blackened" redfish, and it catapulted Paul Prudhomme into the national culinary spotlight, a place that seemed as comfortable to the man from Opelousas as a bayou is to a gator.

Prudhomme was a natural for television. A chef of tremendous girth at the time, he was a colorful man from a colorful place, gregarious and fun-loving; in short, he was an easy interview and his cooking was new, chic, exciting and exotic for its time. As word of blackened redfish spread across the nation, several phenomena occurred. Blackened foods started appearing on menus all over the country with mixed results, Gulf of Mexico redfish (actually a specimen of the drum genus) was overfished to the brink of species extinction, and the lines of people waiting for a seat at K-Paul's and hoping for a glimpse of its suddenly superstar chef stretched down Chartres Street before turning the corner and continuing on Conti.

Prudhomme's staff, mostly family in the restaurant's earliest days, shared the larger-than-life chef's joie de vivre and playful nature, applying stick-on foil stars to customers' faces, the star's color being determined by how clean a customer's plate was once he or she pushed back from the table. The Sensible One was vastly amused by Prudhomme's "star system," reattaching her collection of stars to her driver's license. Her sense of humor, however, wasn't fully appreciated by the state trooper brandishing a radar gun and ticket pad.

Despite the overflowing plates of a new American fusion cuisine and the joy with which it was served, a considerable number of condescending residents dismissed K-Paul's as "okay for tourists" and stayed away. In the midst of runaway success, Prudhomme was in danger of becoming its victim. But instead of growing alarmed by the situation, America's hottest chef considered it an opportunity to grow his flourishing business.

Roughly twenty years ago, the restaurant expanded its capacity to 200 people on two floors, a balcony and a courtyard, resulting in revived favor with the city's local diners. Business is still booming, and most people know that trying to get a table without making a reservation would border on pointless.

It's difficult to believe that K-Paul's is now over thirty-five years old, and perhaps even more difficult to believe that Prudhomme himself is over seventy. Although he no longer cooks daily for customers in the restaurant at 416 Chartres Street, having turned over Executive Chef duties to Paul Miller some years ago, his presence remains regular and, even on those occasions when he's not on the premises, palpable.

In the wake of Katrina's destruction, Prudhomme was adamant about K-Paul's Louisiana Kitchen being one of the first French Quarter restaurants to reopen for business. Knowing that the city's community of musicians was hit just as hard as the restaurant industry, Prudhomme hired jazz musicians to play on the sidewalk at his front door, a practice that still occurs from time to time, now years after the fact.

Over the past quarter century, Prudhomme's circle of operations has expanded. Samples of spices requested by early customers grew into Magic Seasonings Blends®, a spice and sauces company doing business in all 50 states and more than two-dozen nations. His first cookbook, Chef Paul Prudhomme's Louisiana Kitchen, is nearing its 100th printing and has been followed by eight more books. Despite the spice blends, books, television enterprises and image/brand licensing, the true wellspring of the empire continues to come out of the Chartres Street kitchen six nights a week.

It may be misleading to say the cuisine has developed over the past thirty-five years; the more appropriate word is probably "refined." While the relatively short menu is rewritten daily to both reflect and take advantage of the seasonal and regional offerings that give Prudhomme's signature brand of Louisiana cooking its identity, there are always a few basics to be found.

Of course, there is a blackened fish, although these days it's far more likely to be a black drum than a classic redfish (which, incidentally, is also a drum). From time to time, a "bronzed" fish (or other meat), the result of less heat and peppers, appears on the menu. While tamer than their blackened cousins, these dishes are still probably too intense for people gauche enough to ask their waitperson, "Is it spicy?" On that note, most of the food coming out of the Prudhomme/Miller kitchen can certainly be considered to be "full-flavored" if not out-and-out spicy, and those with nervous stomachs or overly delicate digestive systems should really consider going somewhere else and leave the hard-to-get seats for those who will truly appreciate them.

The kitchen notably turns out magnificent etouffées, the "smothered" stews of seafood or chicken cooked with the "trinity" (celery, green pepper and onion) in a smoky roux and served around a scoop of rice.

Prudhomme has been known to say, "Everyone in South Louisiana makes their own special gumbo — and they are all fantastic."

While I'm inclined to disagree, having tasted a few that most assuredly fall short of Chef Paul's level of enthusiasm, it would certainly be an injustice not to highlight the chef's own rendering of what amounts to the national dish of Louisiana. It is rich, smoky and twice as filling as it looks sitting so innocently in a cup.

Interestingly enough, Prudhomme enjoys his gumbo with a scoop of potato salad in it. Figuring "If that's how the master eats it, I'll give it a shot," I did. It was, well, interesting, but not enough for me to make a habit of it, particularly when both elements stand so firmly on their own merits.

Prices at K-Paul's strike some people I know as high, the impression I initially had — at least until my first forkful. At that very moment, any correlation between a handful of nickels and a single bite of manna became sheer folly.

For unsuspecting visitors on a budget, K-Paul's currently offers what they call a "deli lunch." Guests order the dishes at the counter, pick up their plastic knives and forks and search out their table. The food runs from okay to pretty good and the prices are surprising economical for such a nationally-known restaurant, but when considered against the first-rate food and friendly service found at dinner, well, the deli lunch is an insult to both the guest and the sterling reputation of the host. The truth is, dinner at K-Paul's should not be missed, but until they rethink what they're doing, lunch should.

Money isn't really the point at K-Paul's Louisiana Kitchen, and perhaps it never has been. For over a generation, Paul Prudhomme has been more than a chef, spice merchant and cheerleader for a city recovering from the largest disaster in our national history. He's been a true American culinary icon, a Louisiana answer to Frances' Paul Bocuse and Auguste Escoffier, as well as the successor to Julia Child and the acknowledged trailblazer for what has become New Orleans' Golden Age of Chefs.

And how does anyone put a price tag on a national treasure?

K-Paul's Louisiana Kitchen

Louisiana Fusion

419 Chartres Street (between Conti and St. Louis Streets)

Dinner, Monday - Saturday

Lunch, Tuesday - Saturday

All major credit cards are honored and
reservations are emphatically recommended

Cell phones are not allowed in any of the dining rooms

Telephone: (504) 596-2530

Website: www.chefpaul.com

Brigtsen's

It is "Next Step Louisiana Cuisine," its Cajun and Creole heritages unmistakable, but without the preciousness or over-the-top eccentricities of nouvelle cuisine's outer reaches.

Perhaps it's a reflection on our society's celebrity obsession, or maybe it's the number of media outlets that need to keep their fires stoked around the clock, but the true currency of celebrity has been devalued by the increasing number of people who find themselves so pronounced by a fickle public and the breathless media that panders to them.

It's only natural that in a city like New Orleans, where food outstrips even the weather as the leading topic of discussion, chefs would have more cachet than they do in most other places. And while it can be readily argued that New Orleans has far more than its fair share of world-class chefs, the roster of celebrity chefs has become ridiculously long.

These days, lists of New Orleans' celebrity chefs usually have at least eight people on them, and I've seen rosters that include as many as twenty. In an effort to stabilize the hyperbolized currency, I took out a legal pad and a No. 2 Dixon pencil and tried to come up with a list of local chefs deserving to be considered as bona fide celebrities.

I came up with five and a half names, the half being the ubiquitous Emeril Lagasse, and the other five being Paul Prudhomme, Susan Spicer, Frank Brigtsen, Donald Link and John Besh.

Lagasse loses his half point because his far-flung empire of more than a dozen restaurants across the country, his unrelenting television appearances and his corporate assimilation into the Martha Stewart conglomerate have made him more of a visitor to the Crescent City than a resident.

Besh continues to hang on to his full star, despite his growing number of restaurants and increasing television gigs. As of this writing, Besh only has his fingers in eight New Orleans restaurants, the furthest away of which is the charming La Provence across Lake Ponchartrain in Big Branch.

Spicer also flirted with over-expansion several times, but a successful cookbook (Crescent City Cooking), happiness in her later-in-life marriage and the continued runaway demand for "New World Cuisine" at her Creole cottage restaurant, Bayona, and the newer Mondo in Lakeview keep her securely harbored in New Orleans.

While Paul Prudhomme, generally credited as the creator and champion of hybrid Louisiana cuisine, long ago turned the day-to-day operation of K-Paul's Louisiana Kitchen over to executive chef Paul Miller, he remains active in recipe development as well as a high-profile ambassador for post-Katrina New Orleans and indigenous regional ingredients and cuisine.

Donald Link, a chef with deep bayou country roots, gained attention when he partnered with Susan Spicer in creating Herbsaint, the cozy bistro on the St. Charles streetcar tracks. After taking over the restaurant's day-to-day operations, Link also opened the much-discussed Cochon, a combination restaurant and butcher shop specializing in charcuterie. His growing empire expanded again in 2013 with the addition of Peche Seafood Grill, a restaurant featuring wood-grilled fish from Gulf waters.

This brings us to Frank Brigtsen, probably the least known of the celebrity chefs mentioned, due mostly to the fact that he spends the vast majority of his time in the kitchen, doing what a chef should be doing, namely, cooking.

Brigtsen's credentials aren't flashy. A local New Orleans lad, he grew up eating Creole cooking and kicking around city kitchens until he was 24, when he went to work as an apprentice for Paul Prudhomme at Commander's Palace in the middle 1970s. He followed Prudhomme and his late wife when they opened K-Paul's, and served as the initial night chef when the previously lunch-only restaurant started serving dinner.

Prudhomme, a Cajun from Opelousas, is best known for creating blackened redfish and integrating Cajun ingredients into the more urbane Creole cooking then prevalent in New Orleans. This put Brigtsen at the epicenter of the birth of the hybrid Prudhomme referred to as Louisiana Cuisine, and this period would have a profound influence on the up and coming chef.

In 1986, with the help of a loan from his mentor Prudhomme, Frank and his wife, Marna, opened Brigtsen's in a shotgun Creole cottage in the Riverbed section of Uptown New Orleans. Located on a quiet side street away from the city's major convention and tourism centers, the restaurant soon became a bustling local "find" and today remains a busy restaurant with a strong in-town following. The restaurant vaulted into the national spotlight when Frank Brigtsen was named "Best Chef, Southeast" in the 1994 James Beard Awards.

Despite its glittering success and national reputation, the restaurant has chosen to remain small in size, the front of the house (literally) confined in three adjoining rooms with an adjacent shotgun hall alongside. The hall is narrow, and tables pack the dining rooms leaving little room for servers to make their ways through the restaurant. With its most gracious staff, one gets the feeling of being at a lively dinner party in a house too small to hold all the guests. This in and of itself is not an unpleasant situation by any means; rather, it gives the restaurant an intimate "clubby" feeling – that of a friendly local place serving inspired food instead of a starchy "temple of cuisine."

While saying that any single restaurant puts out the best plates of food in New Orleans is an invitation to argument, it isn't difficult to make the case that the best food using local ingredients and techniques is coming out of Frank Brigtsen's kitchen. It is "Next Step Louisiana Cuisine," its Cajun and Creole heritages unmistakable, but without the preciousness or over-the-top eccentricities of nouvelle cuisine's outer reaches.

Main courses are straightforward with restrained flourishes. Consider, if you will, a broiled gulf fish with a crabmeat Parmesan crust, mushrooms and a lemon Mousselline sauce. There's a pan-roasted pork tenderloin with sweet potato dirty rice and pork debris or a panéed rabbit with a sesame crust, spinach and Creole mustard sauce. It is cooking with complimentary regional flavors instead of exotic ingredients selected for contrast. It is home cooking as high art.

While Brigtsen changes his menu with the seasons, his seafood platter, by far the restaurant's most frequently ordered entrée, appears year-round. It is a sampler of six items: grilled drum with crawfish and jalapeño lime sauce; shrimp cornbread with jalapeño smoked corn butter; baked oyster LeRuth with shrimp and crabmeat; baked oyster with fennel, jalapeño shrimp cole slaw, and panéed sea scallop with asparagus purée.

The same virtuosity is reflected in the appetizer menu, which regularly offers as many as a dozen choices from such traditional items as a filé gumbo with rabbit and andouille sausage or a shortcake made of crawfish étouffée with a basil black pepper biscuit, to more adventurous offerings such as oysters and artichoke au gratin or sautéed veal sweetbreads with potato leek cake, mushrooms, capers and lemon roasted garlic butter.

Not too long ago, The Sensible One and I were contemplating pushing back from our table and waddling down the narrow corridor when our server sweet-talked us into splitting a piece of Brigtsen's homemade pecan pie, which had been cited on the Food Network TV program The Best Thing I Ever Ate, by none less than highly regarded Southern cuisine author/connoisseur John T. Edge. While I'm not ready to wholeheartedly agree with Mr. Edge's glittering evaluation, it was one superb piece of pie, and the empty plate looked terribly sad.

Brigtsen's has now been in business well over twenty-five years, quite a long time in the restaurant industry, but seemingly the mere blink of an eye in a city where one family has been running a restaurant for 175 years. Yet in these times, when celebrities are ground out of the media machine like so much sausage, there's something refreshing about a man who has quietly built his reputation in his kitchen instead of by chasing press notice and ceaseless self-promotion.

In a quarter century, Brigtsen has done a mere handful of TV appearances compared to many others in the business, and his empire building was limited to acquiring Charlie's Sea Foods, a family seafood place out on industrial Jefferson Highway.

Charlie's was quite likely the first restaurant to ever serve Brigtsen, who was a neighborhood kid, and he was probably served in a highchair. The place closed after Katrina, and as Brigtsen drove by the boarded-up café every day on the way to his restaurant, the idea to re-open the place became irresistible. The refurbished restaurant re-opened in the summer of 2009 and quickly established a citywide reputation by offering a menu that reflected the restaurant's 1950s origins enhanced by Frank Brigtsen's culinary mastery. Sadly, it all came to an end in 2013 when a greedy landlord tried to negotiate a new lease at extortive rates that infuriated the headstrong Brigtsen to the point he pulled the plug.

So today Brigtsen is devoting all his energies and considerable talents to his flagship restaurant in the shotgun house on Dante Street. If he keeps doing what he's doing at the level he's doing it, one of these years, Frank Brigtsen is destined to become an overnight success.

Brigtsen's
Louisiana Heritage Cuisine
723 Dante Street (next to River Road)
Dinner, Tuesday - Saturday
Reservations are strongly encouraged
All major credit cards are accepted
Telephone: (504) 861-7691
Website: www.brigtsens.com

Bayona

If history serves as any guide, expect further changes in Bayona's menus to reflect the new discoveries Spicer makes in her constantly evolving whirlwind of a life.

For well over twenty-five years, I have been unsuccessfully trying to describe Susan Spicer, the celebrated owner/chef of Bayona in the French Quarter — and that's precisely how I've described her. It's as futile as trying to describe a chameleon by using only one color.

The problem is, just when I think I have her pegged, she changes and what was once a concise assessment is hopelessly out of date. This has been going on for a quarter century, during which I have been regally fed in her restaurants, charmed during our brief howdy-shakes when she makes her rounds, and exasperated when I've tried and failed to replicate her signature pepper jelly glazed duck breast in my own kitchen, armed with her recipe but handicapped by my personal shortage of talent.

Not terribly long ago, I was looking for something to cook and started thumbing through her superb Crescent City Cooking, a cookbook I thought was never going to come out. In her opening paragraph, she reminisces about a warm spring evening in 1979 when she walked in front of the restaurant on Dauphine Street that would ultimately become Bayona. She was on her way to her first cooking job.

I couldn't help but wonder if I were sitting in the restaurant that evening. The restaurant was Maison Pierre, where Cajun/French chef Pierre Lacoste was making a big noise putting out classic French food with Louisiana ingredients. I remember the place as being appropriately fussy and French, but not much else beyond it being the first restaurant where I ever saw a $5,000 bottle on the wine list. (I asked the waiter if anyone had ever bought one and he imperiously told me that the house had sold two, to the same table, in one evening, to two Texans celebrating an oil strike of bonanza proportions.)

Spicer's rise through the kitchen ranks was rapid. In 1986, after a couple of stints in New Orleans and Paris, some extensive traveling and a first executive chef gig at a now defunct restaurant called Savoir Faire, she opened the 40-seat Bistro at Maison de Ville, the French Quarter gem of a hotel where Tennessee Williams is said to have drafted the greater part of A Streetcar Named Desire. To a kitchen so small it included only one oven, four burners and a refrigerator in the alley, Spicer brought her seven short years of experience to a city with a centuries-old reputation as one of America's centers of fine cuisine.

From that point forward, it's been pretty much a Cinderella story for Spicer, minus the cruel stepmother, the glass slipper and the coach that turned into a pumpkin at the stroke of midnight.

The Bistro at Maison de Ville was a success from the beginning, and it was there where Spicer developed such signature dishes as her Cream of Garlic Soup, Grilled Shrimp with Black Bean Cakes and her Seared Duck Breast with Pepper Jelly Glaze. Through the pass-through window opening up to the postage stamp of a kitchen, Chef Spicer could watch people react to the food, which helped her refine current dishes and fine-tune new ones.

It was during her years at Maison De Ville when her original cooking (which she dubbed "New World" cuisine) was wrongly labeled as nouvelle cuisine and she became falsely typecast as a practitioner. This was at a time when nouvelle cuisine was the darling of New York culinary/media circles, and almost any type of cooking using an unusual ingredient was hailed as an innovative example.

Despite the runaway success of both the cuisine and Spicer's reputation, the Bistro at Maison de Ville was owned by the hotel, and entrepreneurial fires were beginning to burn in its headliner chef. One of Spicer's regular customers, Regina Keever offered to back her in a restaurant of her own, and on April Fool's night of 1990, the building which had once housed Maison Pierre opened its doors as Bayona, which was the name of Dauphine Street when New Orleans was under its original Spanish rule. It had been ten-and-one-half years since Susan Spicer admired the building on the way to her first kitchen job.

With a ready-built fan base from her years at the Bistro, a site that had already served as a showcase for one headline chef, and Chef Spicer's penchant for experimentation and invention, it took little time for Bayona to grow into one of New Orleans' most beloved restaurants. Its reputation was cemented when Spicer was named "Best Chef, Southeast" in the 1993 James Beard Awards, the top accolades in the American restaurant industry. By this time, Chef Spicer had become a permanent fixture in discussions of the city's new guard of chefs along with Frank Brigtsen, Emeril Lagasse and other rising stars opening their own restaurants within a few years of each other.

Despite Spicer's success and the attention paid to her cuisine, a clear label for it remained elusive. The "New World" designation gained some traction, but no one could adequately say what it meant. Due to the excesses of self-promoting chefs more concerned with an ingredient's eccentricity than its flavor, the nouvelle cuisine moniker was losing its cachet. Complicating the process was the fact that Spicer was (and remains) an inveterate tinkerer whose cuisine kept evolving as she continued learning.

And perhaps that's the most appropriate name for Spicer's style of cooking – evolutionary. With life changes come cooking changes. Her later in life marriage and an instant family of two children started bringing elements of traditional Louisiana "home cooking" more to the forefront in her recipe development.

Through her collaboration with former partner Donald Link in their very successful restaurant Herbsaint, a new depth and rusticity came into her repertoire. In 2010, she opened another new restaurant, Mondo, in New Orleans' Lakeview neighborhood as a casual alternative to the more formal Bayona. If history serves as any guide, expect further changes in Bayona's menus to reflect the new discoveries Spicer makes in her constantly evolving whirlwind of a life.

A look at the Bayona menu, which changes regularly to take advantage of the seasonal freshness of regionally produced ingredients, and her cookbook gives me the impression that, in most cases, Louisiana is the source of a recipe's central ingredient and the rest of the world is her spice cabinet. This can be found in such dishes as Indian-spiced Turkey Breast with Creamy Red Lentils, Mediterranean Roasted Shrimp with Crispy Risotto Cakes or Shrimp Salad with Fennel and Herbed Cream Cheese on Brioche.

There's also a playful side to Spicer, one of whose most often ordered lunch items is Smoked Duck "PBJ" with Cashew Butter, Pepper Jelly and Apple-Celery Salad, a gourmet take on the old favorite childhood finger food.

Both Bayona's lunch and dinner menus always feature several of the chef's established signature dishes, and fresh-from-market items that have been the beneficiaries of Spicer's dazzling technical skills, intuitiveness, and imagination.

The three smallish rooms and the private patio of the 200-year-old Creole cottage that house Bayona are conducive to civilized conversation without being stuffy. With apricot walls and a profusion of flowers, the white tablecloth restaurant has a formal look, but an unexpectedly informal feel to it. It is not uncommon, late in the evening shift when the kitchen becomes less frenetic, to see Spicer talking to customers and collecting opinions or enjoying a glass of white wine with old friends. Despite the fact that she now has a chef de cuisine overseeing the day-to-day operation of the kitchen, the restaurant is very much "home" to Susan Spicer, and she goes out of her way to make you feel like it's yours as well.

After twenty-plus years of success, the very notion of failure at Bayona is dismissed as preposterous, at least for as long as its energetic chef stays at the helm. But watching Susan Spicer work, as I have since her earliest days at the Bistro at Maison de Ville, one gets the feeling that at least one of her eyes will remain as open to future opportunity as her heart has always been.

For the time being, at least, it's business as usual at Bayona, and business is booming. As for tomorrow or next week or next year, who knows? It's a constantly changing world for Chef Spicer, but there's one thing you can be sure of: If you want a seat at one of her tables, you might want to make reservations several weeks in advance. Because time waits for nobody.

Bayona
New World Cuisine
430 Dauphine Street (between Conti and St. Louis Streets)
Lunch, Wednesday - Saturday
Dinner, Monday - Saturday
All major credit cards accepted and reservations are essential
Telephone: (504) 525-4455
Website: www.bayona.com

Herbsaint

The shrimp was, quite simply, a revelation — still tender and carrying a taste that made me dream of salt air and tall ships, but prominently balanced among the vibrant flavors combined around it. In truth, I have never had better.

How can you help but like stories of people who have bootstrapped their way from the bottom to the top? Case in point: Donald Link, the proprietor and executive chef of Herbsaint, the Louisiana bistro with a decidedly French accent.

A truly local talent, Link's culinary career started at age 15 washing dishes and scrubbing pots in a cramped restaurant scullery. In a story with so many Horatio Alger overtones that no self-respecting Hollywood producer would ever think of filming it, Link kicked around New Orleans kitchens, picking up a trick here and a technique there until he had learned enough skills to start developing a reputation of his own.

In 1993, he headed west to San Francisco, where he attended the Culinary Institute of America and started broadening his horizons in Bay Area restaurants. He returned to New Orleans in 1995, lured by the opportunity to work with Susan Spicer, whose five-year-old French Quarter restaurant, Bayona, was already one of the city's most celebrated places to dine.

After a two-year stint that saw him rise to sous chef at Bayona, Link returned to the Bay Area, working for three more years before once again returning to New Orleans for the opportunity that would make the Crescent City his permanent home. Working with Spicer again, but this time as collaborator and partner, he opened Herbsaint near the heart of New Orleans' Central Business District (CBD).

Within a few years, Spicer left the Herbsaint kitchen and refocused her energies on Bayona, a new cookbook and a less formal restaurant in the city's Lakeview neighborhood. Link continued keeping Herbsaint on track and also expanded his circle of operations to include a stylish new restaurant named Cochon (French for "pig") with an accompanying charcuterie. In 2013, he opened Peche, a noisy quasi-bistro where the emphasis is on fish and which was named the outstanding new American restaurant in the Beard Awards.

Were this indeed a Horatio Alger story, years of hard work, gumption and pluck would have followed, and Herbsaint would have slowly grown into a beloved mainstay of the New Orleans restaurant scene. The truth is, Herbsaint was an overnight sensation, that is, if it took that long at all.

While no one will ever mistake Herbsaint for one of the grand palaces of haute cuisine New Orleans style, there exists a natural synchronicity between the city and the bistro on St. Charles Avenue that is undeniable.

Should you stand across the street and look at Herbsaint, it looks as if someone scattered some tables and chairs in front of a prepossessing, utilitarian building. But as you look longer, you'll notice the tables have white linen tablecloths, while the building has a small gallery and sits behind a stand of leafy trees. The thought that someone might have lifted the whole street corner from a Paris backstreet is almost unavoidable. But every few minutes, the rumble and clatter of an aged green streetcar rolling down historic St. Charles Avenue serves to remind you that you could only be in one American city, and it is "the city that care forgot."

Should you choose to dine inside, Herbsaint is a decidedly understated room. There are some postmodern light fixtures interspersed along the walls that keep the room from feeling blank. A screened fabric depicting tuxedoed jazz musicians subtly blends into the large wall at the back end of the dining room. The bar itself is small and tucked into a corner of the main room, out of traffic and making the place's appellation as a "bar and restaurant" seem reversed. Whether by accident or intent, there is a feeling that the room itself is understated so as not to detract from the main event, which is most assuredly the food.

Like the physical restaurant itself, Herbsaint's cuisine seems to have one foot in France and its other in Louisiana. This is not surprising, considering that both Spicer and Link spent the bulk of their formative years in New Orleans and had the early parts of their careers shaped in restaurants with pronounced Gallic influences. The result is a fusion that is at once local and global, contemporary but with a classical pedigree. Although it has been a number of years since Spicer's departure, the plates at Herbsaint still reflect the natural collaboration of two chefs with comparable backgrounds yet divergent points of view.

The menus for both lunch and dinner are relatively short, with each offering less than a dozen small plates and main courses in addition to soups, salads and sides. These are complemented by two or three off-menu specials that appear to revolve around seasonal specialties.

The language of the menus is both spare and matter of fact, adding an air of elegant simplicity to the cuisine itself. With such offerings as "sautéed Louisiana jumbo shrimp with mushrooms, bacon and spoon bread" and "Muscovy duck leg confit with dirty rice and citrus gastrique," adjectives designed to rouse an appetite would seem not only superfluous, but downright silly.

About the only place the simplicity of the menu language fails is the "antipasto plate" located in the small plates section of the dinner menu. When I ordered it without asking what items or ingredients were included, I had done so with the suspicion it might contain a morsel or two from Link's charcuterie at Cochon, duly famous for using "every part of the pig except the squeal." Once it arrived, the waiter pointed out each item and explained what it was so rapidly that my memory could not absorb, let alone retain the inventory. To my delight, I was served what effectively amounted to a sampling platter from Cochon, containing a petite ramekin of a rabbit terrine, a pâté, shaved slices of a hard sausage and three or four other items with names I can't recall, but the flavors of which I'll not soon forget.

The antipasto plate was an effective curtain-raiser for the Muscovy Duck, which had a deep, smoky flavor evocative of Cajun country, an effect that was amplified by combining the duck with dirty rice, the regional specialty cooked with chicken livers and gizzards, onion, peppers and garlic. The citrus gastrique glazing the duck, a reduction of caramelized sugar and oranges, finished the dish with an inspired whisper of French culinary classicism.

The Sensible One (who has a knack for ordering what I really wanted but didn't know it) opted for a simple green salad, followed by a shrimp risotto with capers in a buttery sauce. The shrimp was, quite simply, a revelation — still tender and carrying a taste that made me dream of salt air and tall ships, but prominently balanced among the vibrant flavors combined around it. In truth, I have never had better.

If anything, balance seems to be the watchword at Herbsaint. From its beginning in 2000, the restaurant has appeared to have effortlessly balanced the culinary classicism of La Belle France with the Cajun and Creole cooking traditions of New Orleans. Herbsaint's exceptional owner/chef Donald Link has balanced the pressures of maintaining the standards not only of such an extraordinary restaurant, but also of Peche, Cochon with its accompanying charcuterie and a private dining facility, Calcasieu, named for the Louisiana parish in which he grew up. In the process, he was named a James Beard Award winner for both his work in the kitchen (Best Chef: Southeast, 2007) and as the author of Real Cajun: Rustic Home Cooking from Donald Link's Louisiana (Best Cookbook, 2009).

Horatio Alger would be mighty proud.

Herbsaint Bar and Restaurant
French-inspired Louisiana
701 St. Charles (at Girod Street)
Lunch served Monday - Friday
Dinner served Monday - Saturday
All major credit cards accepted and
reservations are strongly advised
Telephone: (504) 524-4114
Website: www.herbsaint.com

THE ORIGINATORS

With the city's long-established reputation for culinary inventiveness, it should come as no surprise that New Orleans has served as the birthplace for any number of dishes that are both original and indigenous. What may be more surprising is the number of restaurants, in which the dishes were created, that remain open to this day.

Of course, some of the restaurants where seminal New Orleans foods originated have vanished into the mists of history. Martin Brothers Coffee Stand and Restaurant, the birthplace of the city's iconic poor boy sandwich in 1929, closed years ago. Brennan's, originator of Bananas Foster, fell victim to an internecine feud and a multi-million dollar mountain of debt in 2013 before re-organizing under another member of the Brennan family and re-opening in 2014.

And as for gumbo, well, who knows? Gumbo was probably never invented, but rather it evolved over centuries. There's no question gumbo predates the oldest New Orleans restaurant still in operation today, which is Antoine's, dating back to 1840.

New Orleans has historically been a lightning rod for culinary innovation. This section of the guidebook focuses on four contrasting restaurants that have produced some of the city's most famous foods.

One is a time-frozen grocery store where an enterprising merchant figured out what to do with broken olives in the bottom of barrels and who taught the city to see the humble sandwich in a whole new light.

Another is one of the city's grande dames of cuisine where any number of dishes were first created, but also the kitchen from which one gained such an enthusiastic flowing that it has become a standard in high-end restaurants near the sea.

The third is a neighborhood restaurant where the chef tried to duplicate an entrée a customer had enjoyed in Chicago and failed, producing instead the original version of a quintessentially local dish that has become one of the city's most beloved offerings.

The final restaurant is in the suburbs surrounded by shopping centers, where business was good enough, but once the owner had an idea so simple it's surprising no one had come up with it before, he started selling his new item by the thousands every single day.

There are other restaurants in the city where new dishes are being created every day. There always have been and will be. Who knows from what kitchen the next classic dish will emerge and take an unsuspecting world by storm? It will happen, but chances are it will happen only at the quirky, uneven pace of a city where excitement may boil over but its kitchens more prudently simmer. Stay tuned.

Central Grocery Co.

*The most practical solution is to grab as many paper napkins as you
can get away with, wear old clothes and dig in.*

The old neighborhood is mostly gone now. There's not much that's
French about the historic French Market and, for that matter, there's
not all that much market to it anymore, either.

For more than half a century, the area was New Orleans' "Little
Palermo," but subsequent generations of immigrant Sicilian and Italian
families emigrated first to Mid-City, then the suburbs, leaving the lower
Decatur Street area without much of a cohesive identity.

You'll still find a few trattorias and pizza joints tucked between
Mardi Gras bead shops, Goth bars, boutiques prone to turnover, glorified convenience stores pumping ear-splitting zydeco into the streets
and what appears to be a post-hippie, seemingly lost generation of runaways looking for something – meaning perhaps. You'll find just about
as much authentic Italiana at Olive Garden.

In the middle of all this scrambled identity is an unassuming
storefront. The address is 923 Decatur Street, and the name of the place
couldn't be more generic – Central Grocery Company – but take one
step inside, and you're an ocean away in Palermo.

In the commercialized, Americanized lower half of the French
Quarter, Central Grocery is the last paisano standing. Established in
1906, the storefront grocery market has outlived countless competitors
to gain a special standing in the hearts of New Orleanians.

While it may be true that time has taken its toll on Central Grocery, which keeps chipping away snippets of its charm more for the con-

venience of the people who work there and less for those who shop and buy, you only need to have one foot in the door and you immediately know you've stepped into the Old World, redolent with garlic, cheese, olive oil, salami and so many other heady scents of home cooking, Siciliana style.

The front half of the room, which is the actual grocery store, is a treasure trove for aficionadi della cucina italiana, especially those who revel in its preparation. As generations passed, shelf space became so premium that the store's inventory began expanding vertically instead of horizontally, forcing customers to carefully squeeze their way through tight aisles between tall shelves and display cases of imported Italian foodstuffs. In addition to tins and jars of peppers, olives, squid, anchovies, biscotti and more, you'll find boxes of imported pasta, cases of salamis and cheese, loose beans and lentils sold from the barrel and even the stray dried stockfish from time to time.

At its core, Central may be an old-fashioned grocery store, but the true heartbeat of the place is the muffuletta, the city's signature Italian sandwich, the creation of which is generally credited to the store.

The muffuletta is named for its bread, a crusty round loaf eight or nine inches in diameter. The loaf is stuffed with Capicola ham, Genoa salami, mortadella, and provolone, but what gives the enormous sandwich its true character is the olive salad that's piled upon the meat and cheese. The muffuletta is sold and served in quarters, and a workable rule of thumb is that two of those quarters will usually satisfy anyone this side of a famished longshoreman.

Olive salad harkens back to the days when olives were shipped in wooden barrels of brine. In transit, and even in the store, the weight of the olives in the top of the barrel would crush a number of those at the bottom, rendering them undesirable to the consumers of the day, who were willing to pay full olive price only for full olives. Enterprising grocers would add garlic cloves, capers, parsley and oregano to the broken olives, chop up produce that had gone unsold, and then mix it all in olive oil and red wine vinegar. The result was not only a savory condiment, but also a highly efficient way to make use of inventory otherwise going to waste.

Although olive salad is its most common name, people with a bent for linguistics may find it interesting to know that for the better part of the Twentieth Century, the concoction was generally referred to as "wop salad." While modern cultural sensitivity and political correctness have more or less relegated the term to the lexicological scrap heap, it still appears on some old-line New Orleans menus (most notably at Rocky & Carlo's, a workingman's Italian restaurant in the blue-collar suburb of Chalmette).

To accommodate rushes of business at noontime and the end of the day, the staff at Central Grocery fabricates muffulettas throughout the day. Surprisingly, to a great many people, the longer the sandwich sits unsold, the better it becomes because the olive oil in the salad soaks into the bread itself. Yes, it is messy, but eating a quarter of a muffuletta without having something spill out of the sandwich is an art few people have ever mastered. The most practical solution is to grab as many paper napkins as you can get away with, wear old clothes and dig in.

The back half of Central Grocery provides some very limited areas for eating in, but it is a cramped and soulless place, an obvious after-thought that commandeered valuable and profitable merchandise shelf space.

Far more pleasant it is to pick up a muffuletta and a Barq's root beer, walk a block to the levee and enjoy an impromptu picnic on a bench, watching the ships glide by and feeling the breezes of the Great American River. Or walk two blocks up Decatur Street, grab one of the benches in the circle surrounding the statue of "Old Hickory" in Jackson Square, and listen for the bells of the city's iconic St. Louis Cathedral.

One thing you might want to keep in mind before you enter Central Grocery for the first time is that the people who work there are an inexplicably surly bunch of characters, who take all aspects of play out of playful gruffness as if intent on elevating rudeness to an art form. In fact, it's easier to find more convivial Italian gents on the losing side of a soccer match, driving taxis in Rome or brandishing cabbages when the tenor hits a clinker. Why this may be so eludes me, but I find the best way to get around this is, when they treat me as if I'm nothing but another handful of cash, to ignore them right back.

Before you ask, yes, Central Grocery has muffulettas tightly wrapped in plastic and butcher paper, and ready to go back to the airport with you. It is hardly uncommon to be standing somewhere in a Louis Armstrong New Orleans International concourse and catch a whiff of garlicky olive salad in someone's purse or carry-on as it passes by. (I can't help but wonder what the life expectancy is of a fragrant muffuletta in a jam-packed airplane that's sitting on the tarmac waiting in line to take off or, even worse, for one of those mysterious delays that last an eternity or two.)

Along those same lines, quart jars of olive salad are available for those who don't want the temptation of a whole sandwich under their nose. Perhaps it's just me, but for years, I used to carry them home only to discover the seal was loose enough that oil seeped out onto the label and down the side of the jar, so you might want to make sure the seal is good and tight before you leave the store.

Like most dishes created by New Orleans eateries, the muffuletta has fostered a multitude of imitators not only in the city, but regionally. Many feature a slight variation on ingredients; Napoleon House serves theirs warm, Liuzza's in Mid-City serves a "Frenchuletta" on French bread instead of the traditional Italian loaf, and a few years ago even Emeril Lagasse developed his own muffuletta pizza recipe. As happens in such cases, some of these have attracted their own followings, but those seeking the real deal need only sample l'originale at Central.

And feel free to snarl right back at the surly pagliacco behind the counter.

Central Grocery Company
Muffulettas
923 Decatur Street (between Dumaine and St. Philip Streets)
Open Tuesday – Saturday, 9:00 a.m. – 5:00 p.m.
Major credit cards accepted
Telephone: (504) 523-1620
No website

Antoine's

The good news is that Antoine's is a "must go" for lunch;
the bad is that it's a "must not" for dinner.

"Mr. Demille, I'm ready for my close-up."

As the homicide police look on, Norma Desmond begins to descend the winding staircase. It has been decades since she was a screen idol, but those years have evaporated, and she is once again a certified star, if only in her memory, as she glides down the stairs into the arms of the detectives. Fade to black.

Welcome to Antoine's, not only the oldest restaurant in New Orleans, but also the oldest restaurant in America operated by the same family, which opened the doors in 1840. Like Norma Desmond in Billy Wilder's classic Sunset Boulevard, time has passed by Antoine's, but the restaurant doesn't realize that its glory days will never lie ahead but always behind.

Perhaps it goes without saying that any restaurant in its 175th year of operation will have seen its share of both fat and lean times. Well, maybe not. There aren't a lot of restaurants, particularly in the United States, which have been around long enough to provide a dependable set of statistics. I can, however, say this: In the forty years that I've been kicking around the Crescent City restaurant scene, I've seen Antoine's go from being regarded as a "must go" restaurant to a "must not" and back again.

Within the arc of such a dramatically swinging pendulum, Antoine's seems to be smack dab in the center of the sweep these days. For diners wishing to experience both the historic culinary preparations and disappearing charm of dining in the grand tradition, there's good news and bad news. The good news is that Antoine's is a "must go" for lunch; the bad is that it's a "must not" for dinner.

This may not be so much the fault of the doubtlessly well-intentioned descendants of the Alciatore family, which has owned and operated Antoine's through more than a half-dozen generations, as it is a blind eye toward the potential risks awaiting any institution choosing to stay frozen in a bygone era. Looking at the restaurant industry as a whole, it would seem that old school, elegant dining provides decreasing appeal to an increasing number of potential patrons.

These days, it's difficult not to think of Antoine's more as a shopworn museum than an exemplar of Gilded Age Southern dining. Despite a lengthy and costly restoration in the wake of 2005's Hurricane Katrina, the restaurant already looks tired and tattered around its edges. The place could stand several coats of fresh paint, fresh wallpaper, and enough Windex® to get the glass sparkling on all the framed memorabilia lining the walls.

This is a bigger endeavor than it sounds. With more than a dozen dining rooms, Antoine's is one of the two largest freestanding restaurants in the city, the other being Arnaud's, also located in the French Quarter. Until you take advantage of one of the free tours the restaurant will happily provide during slower hours, it's difficult to imagine the actual size of the operation. At any rate, keeping such a sprawling facility fresh while maintaining its historical integrity appears to be too daunting or costly a task for Antoine's.

That said, Antoine's has a history almost as rich as the city's itself. The list of luminaries who have dined within the restaurant's fabled walls is long enough to keep the most dedicated name-dropper busy. Every U.S. president between Herbert Hoover and George W. Bush has dined at Antoine's. So have Mark Twain, Mick Jagger, the Duke and Duchess of Windsor, Ty Cobb, Elizabeth Taylor, Brad Pitt and Angelina Jolie, Theodore Roosevelt, Henry Kissinger, Sarah Bernhardt, Sydney Poitier, and Tom Cruise just to reel off a quick baker's dozen.

During his historic visit to New Orleans, Pope John Paul II didn't manage to sneak in through the hidden passageway favored by celebrities. Instead, Antoine's prepared all of his meals and delivered them under guard to the archbishop's residence next to St. Louis Cathedral, where the pontiff was lodged.

Most of the celebrity memorabilia adorns the walls of the Large Annex, the largest dining room at Antoine's. On two recent visits, TSI and I were by pure chance seated at the same table in the cavernous room, where we were watched over by a portrait of writer Don Novello in his better-known "Father Guido Sarducci" cassock. The first time, being a fan of the eccentric Novello's brand of satire, I was amused. The second time, I wondered if they were telling me something.

There is more to Antoine's, of course, than its list of glitterati patrons. Over the three separate centuries during which the restaurant has been in operation, its kitchen has created, or been credited for, any number of dishes that have become New Orleans culinary standards. Three of these, for which the Antoine's provenance remains unchallenged, are soufflé potatoes, pompano en papillote and Oysters Rockefeller.

Soufflé potatoes are a remarkably simple dish to prepare in a commercial kitchen, and not all that difficult for a moderately competent home cook to execute in his or her own kitchen. Russet potatoes are rinsed, peeled, sliced razor thin and flash fried at 375°. As fried potatoes rest on paper towels, the oil temperature is raised to a caution-worthy 400 degrees. Once the temperature is reached, the fried potatoes are returned to the oil, wherein they puff into small pillows in roughly fifteen seconds. Once drained, the now "souffléd" potatoes are served with Bernaise sauce on the side. No matter where these little jewels of flavor are prepared, their efficacy as an appetizer or companion to cocktails is yet to be disputed.

Pompano en papillote was created in the Nineteenth Century to celebrate the exploits of a visiting French balloonist. A filet of white pompano, a prized member of the jack family of fish, is placed in an envelope or bag fashioned out of cooking parchment and covered in cream sauce laden with shrimp and crabmeat. Once filled, the envelope is sealed and placed in the oven. As it cooks, the envelope puffs like a balloon. The finished dish is pulled from the oven and served to the guest, bag and all. The bag is sliced open on the diner's plate, releasing its redolent cloud of steam as the contents are revealed.

The most celebrated dish, however, to emerge from the Antoine's kitchen is arguably Oysters Rockefeller, which made its debut in 1889. The original recipe is ostensibly "a closely-guarded secret," that has never left the family or been successfully duplicated. Maybe that's true, but to me it sounds like the kind of marketing flatulence that invariably ends with, "I'd tell you, but then I'd have to kill you."

Oysters Rockefeller isn't all that complicated. It's a raw oyster topped with a green, mousse-like sauce extruded from a pastry bag, sprinkled with breadcrumbs, and then baked. The composition of the green sauce is the so-called secret, but it's been knocked off so often and so well by a legion of chefs that its most valuable ingredient anymore is hyperbole. The color in most versions comes from spinach, although legend has it the house recipe contains no spinach in its checklist of what some people claim consists of up to twenty-three ingredients. Either way, Oysters Rockefeller is a formidable appetizer that certainly deserves the scrutiny of anyone interested in New Orleans heritage dining.

Here are two factoids about Oysters Rockefeller for punishment gluttons with an appetite for esoterica about culinary history. First, the green sauce was originally developed for use with escargot, but a shortage of available French snails and the abundance of plump Louisiana oysters conspired in the subsequent creation of Oysters Rockefeller. Secondly, you get two choices in how the dish was named. Conventional wisdom suggests that the color of the sauce was suggestive of the brighter "greenback" currency in use at the time of both the dish's creation and billionaire John David Rockefeller. The other, which sounds a little invented to me, is that upon first tasting the dish, a customer (with more enthusiasm than descriptive talent) is said to have exclaimed, "These are as rich as Rockefeller." Thank God the dish is better prepared than the simile.

Once stripped of Antoine's history and hype, the food is well crafted if not inspired. The sentence, "It's not as good as it should be," keeps rolling through my brain. It makes me wonder if Antoine's has fallen victim to its heritage. It took Antoine's well over a century to build a reputation bordering on myth and host a VIP guest list lengthy enough to wear out an acre of red carpets. Such a glittering history raises expectations to lofty heights, perhaps unreasonably so. Nonetheless, Antoine's failure to live up to client expectations, however unrealistic those may be, has led to a revised reputation the restaurant may never be able to live down.

The food, most of which is elegant in its presentation, lacks richness and depth. In fact, it's quite often bland. Granted, the world in which renowned trenchermen like Diamond Jim Brady were regarded with awe has given way to one that is health-obsessed, where new generations of calorie counting and sprout sucking fitness fanatics revile real food instead of reveling in it. Perhaps fast food and other factors have deadened the American taste bud and economic forces have impelled Antoine's to follow the leader, but the net result appears to be a diluted version of the opulent, celebratory feasts enjoyed by generations past. How sad.

To be fair, the odds are stacked against Antoine's kitchen. The restaurant's immense size and capacity force its kitchen to plan and execute on an assembly line scale. While such scope doesn't preclude the possibility of getting a far better than average meal, it makes it virtually impossible for the chefs to attend to the nuances necessary to lift a good meal into a great one.

When Hurricane Katrina did an estimated $20 million in damage to Antoine's, it marked the end of the glory days for "the grande dame of St. Louis Street." New economic realities reduced the extensive menu from being a definitive lexicon of "restaurant French" to a stripped-down Cliff's Notes edition of four pages and plenty of white space.

Gentlemen were no longer required to wear neckties and jackets for a meal at Antoine's. While management tried to make light of this by joking that no one still owned such items in the post-Katrina world, the world of civilized dining at Antoine's had waved the white flag.

Katrina or not, the decline of Antoine's was inevitable. The French Quarter, which my mother referred to as the "world's most glorified slum" forty years ago, had been tarnishing for years. Its gradual descent from winking raffishness to leering raunchiness has served to entice local residents toward other fine dining and live music venues throughout the metropolitan area, in effect culturally marooning some of New Orleans' most venerable and civilized establishments. While the city economy's health is fundamentally intertwined with the convention and tourism industry, its pricier restaurants must still depend upon local citizens to remain viable. But with a shrinking number of exceptions, such as Galatoire's and Bayona, the city's residential market is no longer dependable and Antoine's is on the verge of becoming another struggling "middle of the pack" restaurant.

It may be game of Antoine's to put a puckish spin on the relaxation of its dress code, but the old restaurant is simply counting the house, and with all its dining rooms, it's a lot of house. Unfortunate as it may be, it's difficult to find someone with lower fashion standards than the American tourist upon whom Antoine's must rely in order to survive. The grim reality is that it may prove impossible for Antoine's traditions of gracious elegance to remain credible in a roomful of people wearing sneakers and baseball caps.

While it is still possible to enjoy an elegant evening at Antoine's, with ladies and gentlemen dressing like, well, ladies and gentlemen, those doing so may find themselves on the losing side in a war of fashion attrition.

Doubting that Antoine's will ever be able to climb back onto its historic pedestal, The Sensible One and I now limit our sporadic sojourns to lunch, a time when Antoine's can be considered a true value.

During slower times throughout the year, the restaurant offers three-course lunch specials for an amount based upon the year. In 2012, the lunch was $20.12; in 2013, it was $20.13. The food quality is the equal of that served at dinner for considerably higher prices. Better still, limited martinis are available for 25¢ apiece, at lease one price still evocative of the glory days.

Should you start with the oyster trio, and you should indeed consider it, you will be given a card telling you the historic number of the Oysters a la Rockefeller serving you are consuming. For the record, TS1 and I were served 4,027,821 and 4,027,822. Yes, it's a gimmick, but we found it somewhat charming nonetheless. It gave us what the late Eudora Welty called "a sense of place."

In the end, unfortunately, that's what Antoine's is all about.

Antoine's
French Creole
713 St. Louis
(between Bourbon and Royal Streets)
Lunch and dinner, Monday - Saturday
Brunch served Sunday
Reservations recommended and credit cards honored
Telephone: (504) 581-4422
Website: www.antoines.com

Pascal's Manale

*Considering that the provenance of New Orleans Barbecue Shrimp was
a comedy of errors, it should come as no surprise that no one could agree
upon the best way to cook it, either.*

The name is misleading, the history appears to keep revising itself, no
one seems to agree on how the dish is prepared and the most commonly
asked question is, "What's a Manale, anyway?"

Generally regarded as one of the most iconic dishes in the entire
New Orleans Creole-Italian repertoire, Barbecue Shrimp has nothing
to do with barbecue in the way you probably know it. There's no hickory
or mesquite, the sauce isn't tomato based and sweetened with either
brown sugar or molasses, and people in Kansas City and Memphis (and
Texas and the Carolinas) don't argue about whose is best.

This much is known, or at least widely accepted, or maybe sus-
pected: New Orleans Barbecue Shrimp came into being sometime during the mid-1950s in the kitchen of an Italian family restaurant named
Pascal's Manale. Opened in 1913 by one Frank Manale, the Napoleon
Avenue restaurant eventually found its way into the hands of Manale's
nephew, Pascal Radosta, who decided to rename the place after both of
them.

Legend has it that on that fateful evening in the 1950s, one of the
regular customers named Vincent Sutro had just returned from a business trip to Chicago and started singing the praises of a dish he'd eaten
there that, as far as he could remember, had shrimp, butter and a lot of
pepper in it. He asked Pascal's chef, Jake Radosta, if he could make some,
and the chef said he could try.

Chef Radosta went into the kitchen, cooked up something that was as close as he could get to the fellow's vague description and waited while the man tasted it. After a taste or two, the man said it wasn't what he'd eaten in Chicago.

It was better.

Owner Radosta decided to put it on the menu, where it's stayed ever since. No one knows where the name came from. One guess was that this all happened at the point in time when the suburban backyard barbecuing craze was at its zenith and, despite being a misnomer, the name was coined to cash in on the fad. Whether that's true or not, there is a delicious irony about a misrepresented recipe being given a misleading name and still becoming a New Orleans classic.

Considering that the provenance of New Orleans Barbecue Shrimp was a comedy of errors, it should come as no surprise that no one could agree upon the best way to cook it, either.

There are two leading schools of thought on the dish's preparation, and the advocates of each are pompously cocksure that they are correct. The first is that all the ingredients are mixed in a baking dish and put in the oven, and it would not surprise me to learn that this is how the dish was originally prepared in the kitchen at Pascal's Manale. The alternative belief is that the whole process is accomplished on the stovetop in a cast iron skillet.

I have a sneaking hunch both factions are correct, based upon an item I read several years ago that claimed the dish's widespread popularity actually occurred when Paul Prudhomme reworked it for the Brennan family as they prepared to open Mr. B's Bistro in the French Quarter. Prudhomme is a notoriously fast chef well known for cooking with blazing heat at high speeds, and it seems logical that the creator of blackened redfish would rethink a time-honored recipe for ease and speed of preparation in a commercial kitchen.

In writing this, I wanted to be as accurate as possible, so I went to the Internet to do a comprehensive recipe search. There are dozens of them, including numerous ones claiming to be the original recipe, and these "authentic" guidelines cite both cooking techniques. Well, of course they do. All things considered, it wouldn't be real New Orleans-style barbecue shrimp if people could actually agree on its preparation.

But no matter which method of preparation is used, the results are so similar that it takes a true culinary maestro to tell which method was employed. The four driving, traditional flavors are fresh Louisiana shrimp, an exceedingly generous amount of pepper, garlic and enough butter to make a cardiologist scream uncle. Varying recipes call for shrimp stock, Worcestershire, Italian herbs, mint sprigs, Tabasco, white wine, cream and even tomatoes. It is a remarkably flexible dish that readily accommodates any number of personal touches.

There is some disagreement (of course there is) of whether the Louisiana shrimp should be cooked beheaded, peeled and deveined or intact so the fat contained in the shrimp heads can be incorporated into the sauce.

Essential to any preparation is an abundance of crusty French bread to sop up the peppery butter sauce.

When you order barbecue shrimp at Pascal's Manale, a bib is de rigueur. Peeling the shrimp is part of the process, and before the empty plate is taken away, your fingers will be butter-soaked, and possibly wet from licking them (providing no one is looking). Of course you'll look silly; every adult in a bib looks silly, so get over it. One of the latter meals my late father and I had together was at Pascal's Manale, and all these years later, I treasure the memory of our laughing and pointing at each other in our stupid bibs.

Despite the restaurant's age and success, it still retains the aura of a neighborhood, family place. Located on a corner in a shaded, residential area, Pascal's is set in an unobtrusive building on Dryades Street, which also features an old-line steak house named Charlie's, and an unusual structure originally built by the Mexican consulate that now is home to the city's most discreet bed-and-breakfast, complete with a clothing-optional swimming pool.

From the street, you enter a large, wood-paneled waiting room that also houses the restaurant's cocktail area and oyster bar. It's a friendly, lively area, which is good because some people spend a considerable amount of time there. Like many New Orleans neighborhood places, Pascal's has an unwritten policy of moving guests, even those with reservations, down the line when an old friend or regular decides to drop in — and with nearly a century under its belt, the restaurant has an impressive number of friends. While the waits are usually not inordinately long, a little patience is recommended, as are a cocktail and a dozen of the city's better oysters.

There are two medium-sized dining rooms in the place, the motif of one leaning toward sports, and the other seemingly planned to be a "nice" family place, but somehow it ended up looking like the parlor in a cathouse.

Beyond the barbecue shrimp, the menu doesn't stray far from the predictable — some veal dishes, a couple of steaks, seafood grilled or fried. While the shrimp is certainly the headliner at Pascal's, the other dishes are treated as anything other than afterthoughts. It's a good kitchen, the kind anyone has the right to expect of a place that's had nearly a century to work out the kinks.

While the dinnertime mood at Pascal's is jovial, the bibs ludicrous, and the food quality normally hovering somewhere between very good and excellent, lunch at the restaurant offers one of the city's exceptional bargains. A small loaf of French bread is hollowed out, filled with barbecue shrimp swimming in its peppery butter and served as a poor boy sandwich. While bibs are recommended, I've managed the sandwiches with a number of napkins and minimal wardrobe damage.

Summarizing Pascal's Manale is a challenge, at least for me. The food is very, very good, but I can tick off a dozen places that offer better cooking without breaking a sweat. There's a reason for that, and it afflicts several of the city's more legendary kitchens. For more than fifty years, Pascal's has been able to claim itself the originator of New Orleans barbecue shrimp, but with that title comes a tacit obligation not to vary one iota from the recipe as originally conceived and developed. In the meantime, innovative chefs have enjoyed an open field in which to tinker with and tweak the dish, and this has doubtlessly led to some improvements on the original.

Such a fate is not new; it has befallen such venerable culinary institutions as Oysters Rockefeller and soufflé potatoes at Antoine's, the muffuletta as created by Central Grocery Company, the charbroiled oysters developed at Drago's and many others. It begs the question, at what point does a dish as originally developed become a museum piece, a culinary curiosity overshadowed by the creation of a chef enjoying the freedom to explore and innovate? The truth is, there's often a very real difference between a dish that's been invented and one that's been perfected, but they are both of interest to the curious epicure.

For whichever reason you'd consider a visit to Pascal's Manale, historical or hedonistic, chances are you won't be disappointed.

Pascal's Manale
Creole Italian
1838 Napoleon Avenue (at Dryades St.)
Lunch, Monday - Friday
Dinner, Monday through Saturday
All major credit cards accepted
Reservations strongly recommended
Telephone: (504) 895-4877
Website: www.neworleansrestaurants.com/pascalsmanale

Drago's

How many shuckers must it take to pop open nearly eleven thousand oysters in a day? How much butter does it take? Parmesan? Garlic?

Drago's has a long menu, in fact one that's ridiculously long considering that most of the people who come in appear to be ordering one item.

That item is Charbroiled Oysters, a house creation that's become the most widely imitated New Orleans dish since Paul Prudhomme blackened his first redfish and launched a national craze.

The Drago's concept is remarkably simple, so much so that the only thing really remarkable is that no one thought of it until 1993, when second generation manager Tommy Cvitanovich poured some house barbecue drumfish sauce (butter, garlic and a handful of herbs) over some oysters on the half shell, sprinkled a little parmesan cheese on top and slapped it on the charcoal grill. The finished oysters are served in a generous amount of the sauce with enough ficelles to sop it up.

These days, according to the company website, the restaurant's two locations put out about 900 dozen charbroiled oysters on a busy day. Stop and think, and the math becomes staggering. How many shuckers must it take to pop open nearly eleven thousand oysters in a day? How much butter does it take? Parmesan? Garlic? On the sales side of the equation, how many family-owned restaurants with only two locales gross several million a year? On one item?

In light of the restaurant's runaway success since 1993, it's difficult to put the previous twenty-four years of Drago's operations in proper context. When Drago and Klara Cvitanovich first opened for business in 1969, they were just another mom-and-pop team trying to carve out a niche in the Metairie family restaurant marketplace, although their Croatian heritage gave them an inside track.

Since settling in Louisiana and along the Mississippi Gulf Coast in the middle of the Nineteenth Century, Croatian-Americans have been the backbone of the region's oystering business. From seeding to harvesting, shucking and serving, successive generations of Croatians have been a mainstay of the industry, and it has long been believed, whether warranted or not, that the most preferred oysters have been held in reserve for "family" eateries.

Success for Croatians in the New Orleans restaurant industry has become a tradition. Until the restaurant's sale in 2011, the Vodanovich family operated Bozo's (a Croatian nickname for "Christopher") from the day the venerable seafood house opened in 1928. Uglesich's opened in 1924 as a sandwich shop, but by the time it closed in May of 2005, three months before Hurricane Katrina, the ten-table restaurant in an iffy part of Central City had developed a national reputation for innovative seafood recipes. The Vojkovich family opened Crescent City Steakhouse in the city's Seventh Ward in 1934, and with the exception of a few JazzFest posters on the wall, the city's oldest family-operated steakhouse looks very much the same as it did on opening night.

Located on a sleepy side street not far from New Orleans' largest shopping center, Drago's steadily built an enviable family business trade. Despite numerous expansions to the building and seemingly endless re-decoration, what is now a major enterprise with more than three hundred employees manages to retain the family attitude and ambience that stretches back over forty years to the restaurant's beginning. This is reflected in the menu's comparative length and in the demeanor of the wait staff, some of whom look experienced enough to have their service stretch back to Day One.

The foundation of the lengthy menu, not surprisingly is local seafood, cooked in any number of ways. These are augmented by prime rib, veal, chicken, pasta dishes and one incongruous item called "Shuckee Duckee," a blackened duck breast served over linguini and finished with oysters in a cream sauce. The entrees, and there are eighteen of them listed as specials, tend to run toward the complex in their preparation, the simplest being the traditional prime rib plate and the most complex appearing to be the Barbecue Drumfish (according to the menu a "Drumfish filet, lightly seasoned with fresh herbs, butter, and garlic grilled over an open flame. Served with fresh crabmeat and shrimp dressing, then topped with a crabmeat cream sauce").

Despite such a panoply of entrees, Drago's makes a point of emphasizing its live Maine lobsters. The live boilers start at a pound and go to well over three (listed as "Super Stud" on the menu), and the house also serves them stuffed or sauced three different ways. From my point of view as a frequent visitor, there seems something slightly anomalous about being in one of the world's legendary seafood cities and ordering lobster from the frigid waters north of Boston, but I suppose even the denizens of paradise hanker for change from time to time.

In the name of full disclosure, I must tell you that I know very little about the food beyond the Charbroiled Oysters except what I read on the menu and observe when the occasional plate of something besides the oysters passes by on its way to another table.

What's the point?

When we visit Drago's, The Sensible One and I always start with a dozen each of charbroiled oysters before ordering another half dozen or more. Our record is five dozen, and the thing that makes me happiest is that the number of oysters presented is always divisible by two, which prevents an eye-to-eye showdown over the final bivalve and undoubtedly less than chivalrous behavior on my part.

In recent years, Drago's has opened a second operation in the Hilton Riverside at the foot of Poydras Street. The food may be the same, but the place isn't. In fact, compared to the original location, it's remarkably sterile. While the original retains the feel of a flourishing family business, the Hilton location retains the feel of, well, a Hilton.

For some visitors, food is food, a slightly interesting single step above fuel, and ambience is a minor concern. To the true experience seeker, the physical surroundings and service are as integral parts of a restaurant's total flavor as the food. The Hilton's downtown location, a couple of blocks from the French Quarter, is certainly more convenient for most visitors to the city. Whether or not ambient authenticity is important to you as a visitor is truly a matter of choice; either way, the oysters are great.

The runaway success of Drago's charbroiled oysters has led, of course, to any number of restaurants imitating the dish, as happens with any new and successful recipe. In some cases, a dish is invented by one chef, but perfected by another. TSi and I have a tendency to want to try a dish in its original configuration, which sends us searching for its point of origin. Perhaps we're missing something newer and improved, but in the case of charbroiled oysters, we find ourselves returning time and again to the source — because improving on perfection is a mighty tall order.

Drago's Seafood Restaurant
Charbroileld Oysters
3232 N. Arnoult Rd, Metairie
Lunch and dinner, Monday — Saturday
All major credit cards honored
No reservations
Telephone: (504) 888-9254
Website: www.dragosrestaurant.com

Clancy's

*To take absolutely nothing away from Clancy's, its inspiration is
so transparently based upon one of the grand temples of Creole cuisine
they could have named the place "Galatoire's Lite."*

When Anthony Uglesich closed his namesake restaurant three months
before Hurricane Katrina ravaged New Orleans, I was more distraught
than I normally would be by the closing of a Crescent City dining establishment.

Hell, I couldn't blame the man. "Mr. Ant'ny" had gone to work
for his father there some fifty years before. He'd watched the neighborhood go from working class to seed, his knees were shot from spending
a half-century on his feet and, try as he might, he couldn't find a buyer
who'd be willing to actually work at the tumbledown joint.

The reason for my anguish was that the soft-shell crabs so simply
fried and served by Uglesich's were nothing less than the dish's gold standard. Prior to my fortuitous discovery of Uglesich's, I had found the
source for such a glittering designation to be an old Mom-and-Pop
called Crechale's in, of all places, Jackson, Mississippi.

Somehow, these two places had led me to believe that the only way
to find good soft-shells was to look around for out-of-the-way places
that had been around for at least several generations. Now, after ten
wilderness years of sampling New Orleans soft-shell crabs – fried,
sautéed and in poor boy sandwiches – I've once again found the elusive
gold standard, and wouldn't you know it, it's an old, out-of-the-way
place that's been around for more than a century.

The old restaurant that has evolved into the new standard-bearer is Clancy's, located at the corner of Annunciation and Webster streets in a quiet, Uptown neighborhood where the houses are more tasteful than grand. For twenty-five years, Clancy's has been an upscale restaurant, but in an American city that will celebrate its 300th birthday in less than five years, that's merely the blink of an eye.

The simple frame building has been around since the beginning of the Twentieth Century and, in that time, it has sometimes housed a bar, sometimes a neighborhood café and sometimes a white tablecloth restaurant. Sometimes, like today, it's all three.

Shortly after the end of World War II, the place was bought by a couple named Ed and Betty Clancy, who operated it as a neighborhood bar and poor boy shop virtually inseparable from the similar businesses that seemed to set up shop on every other corner of the Crescent City.

In 1983, after more than thirty years of minding the store and with no heirs to whom the tavern cum café could be passed, the Clancys sold the business and the building to three businessmen who morphed the bar and restaurant into its current incarnation. About the only thing that didn't change was the name, which was probably just as well. After all, Clancy's is a grand Irish name for a saloon, and certainly an easier way to answer the telephone than with the names of the trio of new owners ("Good evening. Thank you for calling Slattern, Livaudais and Wagner's"). Four years later, the trio sold out to Brad Hollingsworth, who had bootstrapped his way from the kitchen up to ownership and who remains one of the restaurant's partners to this day.

Clancy's ultra-slick website proclaims the restaurant as "one of the first Creole Bistros which revolutionized the New Orleans dining scene in the 1980s and became a template for the most prevalent restaurant style in New Orleans today." As a recovering advertising copywriter myself, I certainly recognize overcooked prose when I smell it, and I can only hope such an egregious example of hyperbole is a mere byproduct of unbridled corporate enthusiasm than a deliberate overlooking of accepted culinary history. To take absolutely nothing away from Clancy's, its inspiration is so transparently based upon one of the grand temples of Creole cuisine they could have named the place "Galatoire's Lite."

The similarities between the two establishments are remarkable. Both are considerably less fussy than some of the grand old dowager restaurants with origins in times when the world was illuminated by gaslight. You'll find archetypical bentwood furniture, understated crockery and flatware, tuxedoed wait staffs with professional demeanors that border upon the patrician, the mirrors and brass coat hooks on the walls. When the linen wrapped loaf of bread arrived at the table at the start of the meal, I would have sworn it came from the same bakery that purveys to Galatoire's.

There are two key areas, however, in which the two restaurants diverge; the first being their physical layouts, and the second being the stages of each cuisine's development.

Instead of one substantial dining room, Clancy's main room accommodates a modest thirteen tables, while another four tables occupy a subdued wine room separated by a galley-style bar containing about a dozen barstools. Additionally, there are several smaller upstairs rooms, each painted a deep green and the largest of which is dominated by a wall-sized wine rack. These smaller venues afford separate intimacies that cannot be found in the table-hopping, cocktail party din of the considerably more voluminous Galatoire's.

In terms of cuisine, the thirty-year-old Clancy's has the advantage of relative youth over its 110-year-old forerunner. While both kitchens have their roots in classic Creole cuisine, the cooking staff at Galatoire's is virtually handcuffed by a hidebound clientele who greet the slightest change from the time-honored with at least suspicion if not outright scorn. By contrast, the food at Clancy's is more contemporary, yet not so much revolutionary as evolutionary. New ideas, ingredients, and techniques are integrated into the cooking, without straying into the eccentric self-indulgences that have proven the downfall of many overly "creative" albeit lesser talented chefs.

Take, for example, the signature soft-shell crab. Before it is fried, it is smoked, which enhances the sweetness of the crabmeat while not overpowering it. On the surface, this is a remarkably simple idea, but in the intensity of a working commercial kitchen there comes a certain degree of difficulty in taking a foodstuff as intrinsically delicate as a soft-shell crab, essentially cooking it twice and not having it come out with the consistency of a pooch's chew toy. Yet the smoked soft-shell produced by Clancy's is not only sweet and smoky, but still exceptionally moist as well, and the sweetness becomes further enhanced once the whole thing is covered with large pieces of additional, premium crabmeat.

A fried oyster appetizer, another offering easily rubberized by lack of attention, retains its moistness and is lifted beyond the prosaic by the inspired addition of melted Brie. A seared yet tender sea scallop is enhanced by foie gras and an intense port reduction. All of this is serious cooking, based in classical Creole French ingredients and techniques, and flawlessly produced in what amounts to little more than a ramped-up neighborhood bistro.

While the owners of Clancy's may take a small degree of umbrage to the comparison to Galatoire's, or even take it as a compliment that it left-handed instead of right-minded, I cannot take credit for it. A reader of an earlier edition of this guidebook, in urging me to investigate Clancy's referred to it as "the Uptown Galatoire's," and I've heard others draw the same conclusion over the years. It truly is an almost unassailable truth — and so is this:

If New Orleans has a dirty little secret to the outside world, it's that there exists a misanthropic element within the Uptown population that takes great pride in its muttered disdain for the French Quarter and the throngs of hungry visitors who make tourism the city's largest industry following the Mississippi River port. What I find ironic is that it's these selfsame hard-shelled crabs who make a table at the contemporized clone of Galatoire's traditions one of the toughest reservations in town.

Now that I know about Clancy's, I'm going to do all I can to make it even tougher for those hard-boiled bastards to reserve a table, and I encourage you to do the same.

Clancy's

Creole French

6100 Annunciation Street (at Webster)
Dinner, Monday – Saturday
Lunch, Thursday and Friday
Credit cards honored
Reservations emphatically recommended
Telephone: (504) 895-11112
Website: www.clancysneworleans.com

Rocky & Carlo's

I couldn't help but laugh and told the woman I'd hate to see a small order. "
That is a small order," she said. "Yours."

"Nothing exceeds like excess."

That would certainly be a more apt, not to mention politically correct, slogan for Rocky & Carlo's than "Ladies Invited," but one visit to the Chalmette eatery will make it clear that political correctness is the least of their concerns.

Even after a major renovation following a 2013 fire that caused enough damage to shutter the restaurant for six months, the place remains a throwback to 1965, when Rocky & Carlo's first opened its doors. At the time, there was nothing uncommon about "men only" taverns and that doesn't seem to bother their customers one bit. In fact, looking at the current clientele, it might be a safe bet that a lot of them would like to see those days return.

I'd heard about the restaurant for a good many of its fifty years, usually about their macaroni and cheese, which has developed an almost mythic status in New Orleans. Somehow I'd never gotten around to visiting the neighborhood around lunchtime or anywhere near the dinner hour. If you've ever spent any time in Chalmette, Louisiana, you already understand why.

To get to Chalmette from the French Quarter, one has to pass through the Marigny, Bywater, the wasteland that was once the Lower Ninth Ward and Arabi. Each neighborhood is worse than the one before, at least until you get to Arabi, a town with all the charm of a neglected industrial park. Once you leave Arabi, you drive around a bend and then aim your headlights down a stick-straight stretch of highway that might politely be described as "featureless."

There is, however, one feature along the bleak stretch of highway that seems as out of place as a Baptist preacher at a craps table. It is a tall white obelisk marking the field and historic trench where the Battle of New Orleans took place two hundred years ago. Should you have a spare hour, the battlefield is far more interesting than it looks from the highway, especially if you watch the surprisingly well-done audiovisual presentations in the Visitors Center (I say that because I'm always thunderstruck when the federal government manages to do anything well).

Beyond an excursion to the battlefield, there's not a lot of reason to visit Chalmette. Aside from the industrial highway running alongside the Mississippi River, Chalmette is just another blue-collar suburb featuring middle class housing, chain restaurants, big box stores and a shopping mall or two. Every American city of any size has a bedroom community that becomes the butt of local jokes, and in New Orleans, Chalmette often fills that role.

"Chalmation Nation," as it's jokingly referred to by it residents, is a city that works as much on brute force as brainpower. The people work hard, eat hearty and judging by the lengthy lines that often form for both lunch and dinner, it looks like all of them eat at Rocky & Carlo's.

And they eat damned well.

There is no artifice at Rocky & Carlo's. The food, dished up in portions gargantuan enough to send Fred Flintstone home toting a to-go box, is Louisiana home cooking with a Sicilian accent and served in a cavernous room with all the ambient *je ne sais quoi* of a cafeteria.

A first visit to Rocky & Carlo's can prove both confusing and frustrating because from the outset it's apparent that the place runs by its own rules and everyone in the room knows them except you.

Here's how it works, at least as near as I can tell. You start next to the restrooms at the back of the house, where you'll find a home-decorated chalkboard listing specials ranging from veal parmesan to "wop salad" and the ubiquitous mac-and-cheese. Next is a whiteboard where the daily specials are scrawled, it seems, with impressive velocity but little regard for such a pesky detail as proper spelling.

Your next stop is at a cafeteria counter, where a comprehensive menu is taped to the aluminum shelf in front of the glass protecting a steam table brimming with bubbling and gurgling home cooking that resembles nothing you've seen on the boards. One of the gaggle of pleasant women of indeterminate ages stands behind the counter, order pad in hand. It's showtime at Rocky & Carlo's.

By the time TSI and I made it to that point, we were confused beyond indecision. After several false starts, we decided to share a small order of the vaunted macaroni, an order of onion rings available only in a single size and a fried shrimp poor boy, figuring if we were still hungry we could get one of the colossal, gooey desserts I had spied in a refrigerated case beside the cafeteria line.

When TSI wandered off to stake a claim on one of the smaller tables in the cavernous dining room (a four-top), I paid and waited for drinks at the cash register. While I was standing there, one of the workers set a gigantic oval platter of macaroni on the counter, and I marveled at the excessive size of one of the restaurant's large orders, which looked like it could easily feed six or seven famished longshoremen.

I couldn't help but laugh and told the woman I'd hate to see a small order. "That is a small order," she said. "Yours."

To say the order was large was an understatement, as evidenced by the fact that it and two drinks served in plastic stadium cups (duly inscribed "Ladies Invited") covered the better part of a standard cafeteria tray.

I had no sooner put it down on the table than the pleasant woman who had taken our order at the counter followed with the onion rings, which dwarfed the platter of macaroni, and the ten-inch poor boy so loaded that fried shrimp were falling out of the sides of the French bread. Once the server had left the table and we could get a good look at everything, the ten-inch poor boy looked like half a leftover Parker House roll next to the mountains of macaroni and rings.

The onion rings were cut skinny enough to be limp, a manner Chef Paul Prudhomme calls "frings." TS1, whose passion about rings is such that I defer to her judgment, declared them among the top three in all of New Orleans, not faint praise in a city where there are very few menus that don't include them as an appetizer.

Since I've spent the last couple of years combing the city for the best shrimp and roast beef poor boys, I wasn't expecting too much from a semi-Sicilian cafeteria specializing in lunches that drip over the edges of their plates. I should have known better. The shrimp were fresh-out-of-the-Gulf sweet, the batter was appropriately crisp and they were every bit as large as those served at Parkway Bakery & Tavern, the Mid-City joint widely regarded as the gold standard for seafood poor boys.

Had I been looking in good and earnest for a Parkway rival, I can assure you that Chalmette wouldn't have been the first destination on my search itinerary, but that's one of the culinary joys of New Orleans. Great cooking abounds in "the City that Care Forgot," and as long as you enter with an open mind and a finely tuned fork, you never know behind which door you'll find it.

As these things work out, while I was bowled over by the quality of the frings and shrimp, the main reason I searched out Rocky & Carlo's, the widely hailed macaroni and cheese turned out to be a disappointment (although assuredly not in size). This wasn't new territory for me, because the same thing happened to me at Jack Dempsey's, a family seafood joint in the Bywater neighborhood where the mac-and-cheese is equally revered. I think I might like good macaroni almost as much as the next guy, but it may be that the basics of the dish don't lend themselves to superlatives.

The macaroni and cheese at Rocky & Carlo's features unusually long, hollow noodles called *perciatelli* in a gooey, rich sauce dominated by ricotta and cheddar cheeses. Beyond the noodles' thickness and length, it's pretty standard stuff. Several generous shakes of black pepper or a shot of Tabasco gave it a helpful lift. While it's perfectly fine food, I fear the surrounding hype that led us to Chalmette in the first place also may have led us to unrealistic expectations.

I wouldn't let that deter you, however, from schlepping out to Chalmette for lunch or dinner, particularly if you're looking for places "where the locals eat."

You'll see workmen grimy enough to look like they just crawled out of a pipe, which is more than possible in such an industrial area.

I also noticed two guys in short-sleeved dress shirt and neckties hovering over a laptop and overflowing plates of veal parmesan and meatloaf.

The local chapter of the Kiwanis Club meets there every Tuesday at noon.

Truth is, Rocky & Carlo's is about as local as it gets, and it doesn't need a new, all-to-often deceptive marketing slogan.

Besides, they already have a perfectly fine one in "Ladies Invited."

Rocky & Carlo's
Blue-collar cuisine
613 West St. Bernard Highway, Chalmette
Lunch and Dinner, Tuesday – Saturday
No reservations
Credit cards honored
Telephone: (504) 279-8323
No website

Café 615 ("Da Wabbit")

*The food becomes more aggressive at night,
but stays true to its Louisiana working class roots.*

Da Wabbit isn't the real name of the place except to all the people who go there, and a lot of people do.

The restaurant first opened as a drive-in café in 1949, located on one of the main drags in Gretna, a working-class community across the Mississippi River from the city proper. Sixty-six years later, Da Wabbit hasn't moved, but the main drag has. And that seems to suit the people of Gretna just fine.

Roughly a dozen years ago, a new owner came in and took over Da Wabbit, which served decent food but had degenerated into a blue-collar roadhouse that served rivers of cold beer and kept a very busy card table in the back room. The new owner spiffed up the old roadhouse, upgraded the food, chucked the card table, restored some respectability and, as a final signal that things had changed, re-named the place "Cafe 615 Home of Da Wabbit."

Well, the new name never really took, except perhaps as a line of demarcation between people who know better and those who don't. Naturally, I heard about Da Wabbit from my running buddy, Slider Bob, a man with a finely tuned nose for good hot food and better cold beer. Not too long ago, Slider took it on himself to become an unofficial chamber of commerce for both Gretna and nearby Algiers Point, and when it comes to Da Wabbit, his drum beating can be deafening. I had to see the reason for his rabid enthusiasm and now that I have, call me a convert.

Da Wabbit caters to the 95% of New Orleanians who get up every morning, go to the office or the wharf, drive cabs, pay taxes, go to Mass, drop the kids off at school and go out of their way to fit in rather than stand out. The place serves straightforward, Louisiana Mainstream cooking and seems content to repel the remaining, outspoken five percent — those culinary thrill-seekers who confuse eccentricity with creativity, see the kitchen as a playing field for curious games of ingredient one-upmanship, and never hear a name they wouldn't drop.

Until a new portico was built on the front of the building in 2012, one look at the place would tell you that decorators never descended upon it. The main room has plain beige walls above a chair rail and a rusty red wall below. There are framed posters from Gretna festivals interspersed with seasonal décor for such observed New Orleans holidays as Christmas, Mardi Gras and Saints Football. The front room is still a small, dark bar with six tables, but these days it seems to be utilized more for customer spillover than as a hard-pouring saloon.

Things move quickly at Da Wabbit, and I don't know if that's because the owner is trying to get the tables to turn over quickly, or maybe the people who come to Da Wabbit for dinner like to grab, gulp and git. On our maiden visit, after being slightly startled by how quickly we were asked if we were ready to order, The Sensible One and I never felt rushed or herded. The young woman serving us was well scrubbed and most pleasant, and it struck me that it probably wasn't all that long ago that she was babysitting the kids of most of the people in the room. Just the same, she was top-notch as a server and her memory was impressive. It truly requires a prodigious memory to work at Da Wabbit. The menu is long, and it seems like the list of items on the whiteboard of a dozen or more specials is even longer, yet our server ticked her way down the list without skipping a beat.

Beyond the sheer number of items on the menu and the board, there are no real surprises. During lunch, you'll find the usual array of sandwiches, soups, salads, and plate lunches. On Thursday, one of the daily specials is white beans and rice with smothered rabbit, while the daily house special is Da Wabbit Hamburger Steak. Go figure. Somehow it makes sense here.

The food becomes more aggressive at night, but stays true to its Louisiana working class roots. It's heavy on seafood – fried (of course), grilled or broiled – and there's the usual pork, chicken, and steak. Everything, with the possible exception of the steak, seems to be cooked in a variety of ways and finished in a wide array of sauces; the most common seems to be a variation of buttery cream sauce containing either shrimp or crawfish. If one word describes the cooking to working class folks in Louisiana, it would probably be "familiar." The Sensible One prefers to call it "comfort," and when you consider the aforementioned house specialty is a hamburger steak smothered in mushrooms and onions, she makes a pretty valid point.

Due to the length of the specials list, we had to ask our server to go through it a second time, which she did, surprisingly cheerfully at that. While she went through the list, I found myself changing my mind about every three items, and totally forgot that I was going to order the fried chicken, to which I'd been tipped off by several blogs and articles.

As things turned out following the recitation, we split an off-the-menu appetizer of a half dozen panéed frog legs served on a garlicky bed of onions, red bell peppers, black olives and capers sautéed in a butter sauce with a strong Sicilian overtones. Beyond being enjoyable, it was certainly enough for the two of us.

The Sensible One ordered crawfish étouffée paired with fried catfish filets. What ultimately arrived we could have easily split and contentedly waddled away. Even though crawfish étouffée is one of the mainstays of Cajun cooking, in truth it can be a complex dish loaded with potential pitfalls for chefs of any level. Da Wabbit's version of the old classic was delightful – a balanced blend of smoky roux, fresh seafood and layers of spice that, while definitely peppery, didn't require a fire extinguisher as a washdown.

Her catfish was just fine. It was fried catfish, for Pete's sake, a food so simple it would be a waste of perfectly useful adjectives to point out anything beyond the fact that the filets were thinner than many, but thicker than the gold standard thin catfish served some forty-five miles away at Middendorf's.

After bouts with indecision following my forgetting about the much-praised fried chicken, I finally ordered Soft-Shell Crab Orleans – but only after a full explanation. Over the years, I've learned that the names given to dishes are essentially meaningless in a city brimming with chefs whose cooking styles identify them as everything ranging from old school conservatives to freewheeling daredevils. What arrived was a traditionally fried soft-shell on a slab of grilled garlic toast and covered with a crawfish, cream, and cheese sauce. Also on the plate were a side of pasta covered with the sauce, and some green beans that were grilled with other vegetables suspiciously similar to those that had come with the frog leg appetizer.

It was here where I encountered the one disappointment in what came out of Da Wabbit's kitchen. While the sauce exquisitely yet subtly complimented the soft-shell crab, when ladled over pasta there was an overpowering flavor of cheese that tasted more processed than natural. The Sensible One said it tasted like Velveeta™ and while I'm not willing to be quite that disparaging, it was the only misstep in what was otherwise a superb meal.

People looking for a hip, urban dining experience might do well to avoid Da Wabbit. Of course, it can probably be said that people looking for a hip, urban experience of any sort might want to avoid New Orleans altogether. Despite the city's well-deserved reputation for partying every bit as hard as it works, if not harder, the West Bank very much remains a working class city to its residents, and when it comes to cooking, most residents find more comfort in the trailing edge of a chef's knife than they do in its cutting edge.

Da Wabbit unapologetically and brilliantly caters to its West Bank clientele and, as the West Bank begins to finally take on its first whispers of social cachet, more people are discovering places that have somehow remained undiscovered for decades.

For visitors who are looking for a truly reflective dining experience instead of some quick buck artist's pre-packaged version of warmed-over clichés, there are a lot of worse places to start than Da Wabbit. Yes, it's real name may be "Café 615 Home of Da Wabbit" these days, but this is New Orleans, chere, and very few things here are ever exactly what they appear to be, with one possible exception being Da Wabbit. Thank goodness.

NOTE: Since this piece was first written, The Sensible One and I have made many trips to Da Wabbit. My memory finally cleared up, and the fried chicken is terrific.

Café 615 ("Da Wabbit")
Louisiana Mainstream
615 Kepler Street, Gretna
Lunch and dinner, Monday – Friday
Dinner only on Saturday
Telephone: (504) 365-1225
No website

Katie's

The reasons for Katie's post-Katrina success and snowballing reputation are the cooking itself and a sharp eye for the details that lift the entire restaurant experience another level or two.

It's only natural, I suppose, that visitors to New Orleans spend most of their time in and around the picturesque French Quarter. It's perhaps equally natural, even if somewhat less than hospitable, for natives to neglect telling visitors about their favorite places outside the "visitors zone."

A good example of such a place might be Katie's, ostensibly a neighborhood place in Mid-City, but one you might expect in a more upscale neighborhood – maybe on St. Charles between Napoleon Avenue and Audubon Park, or nestled between a couple of chi-chi boutiques on one of the better blocks of Magazine Street.

Mid-City started out as boondocks, but the city grew out to it in the latter years of the Nineteenth Century, a fair part of that growth coming as significant portions the city's Italian/Sicilian emigrant population was integrated and ultimately accepted into the emerging middle class. To this day, there remains a strong Italian influence in the area, as evidenced in the neighborhood restaurants. The most famous of these is Mandina's, but within blocks are Liuzza's, Venezia and Angelo Brocato's Fine Italian Ice Creams & Pastries. (The youngest of these is Venezia, which was opened more than a half century ago in 1957.)

Katie's has the kind of quirky history I've come to expect from one of the city's almost countless neighborhood restaurants. The place was first opened by Leo Leininger as a fresh, new career start after he became one of the many casualties from the 1984 bust of Louisiana's oil industry. The timing of his October 1984 opening is interesting for another reason as well. It was the last month of the 1984 World's Fair.

While that 1984 expo turned out to be a $350,000,000 financial albatross with governmental intervention required for completion of its run, it lifted the city's spirits and released a great wave of optimism throughout the community. The French Quarter went through one of its periodic gussying-up phases, the hospitality industry boomed and the fair's site itself served as a revitalizing urban renewal project for the Central Business District riverfront and the crumbling Warehouse District that had overgrown the site of the city's old railroad yards.

Combine Leo Leininger's late-in-life career change with the unjustified, myopic optimism stemming from the fair and the result is a predictable recipe for financial catastrophe, but somehow the restaurant hung in and survived, becoming an integral part of the Mid-City landscape. The enormous amount of hard work and determination it takes to launch a new restaurant based more upon hope than actual experience exacted a substantial toll from its owner and within four years, Leininger died. His family continued to operate Katie's for another six years before selling to the more experienced Craig family, who still run the business with another partner to this day.

At this point, many a story would fast forward to "happily ever after," but in 2005, Katie's Mid-City location took seven feet of water from Katrina and what wasn't immediately destroyed in the hurricane's subsequent flooding was carted off by the hordes of looters who showed up in the aftermath. To make matters even worse, the insurance settlement was barely enough to cover the reconstruction of the building's second floor, where owner Scot Craig made his home above the restaurant.

Determined to rebuild a better, more up-to-date Katie's, Craig spent the four-and-one-half years rethinking, rebuilding and reworking the entire operation. A genuine Brooklyn-style pizza stone oven was added and the entire kitchen was outfitted with top-shelf quality equipment. A glass block wall separating the bar from the restaurant proper, gives the entryway a vintage neighborhood restaurant appearance that helps establish an ambience that suits not only the building, but the surrounding environs as well.

Katie's reopened in the spring of 2010 and has become increasingly busy in the same amount of time it takes word-of-mouth to spread throughout New Orleans. To a large degree, family members, including Scot Craig's ageless mother, Mary, who still greets customers at the door as she has been doing since 1994, staff the place. The staff's mutual affection and sense of family became apparent on a recent visit, when Mary arrived twenty minutes late because of a flat tire. Upon her arrival, the restaurant's business ground to a complete halt as every staff member gathered around to check on the house matriarch. It was an endearing moment that no customer appeared to mind, and it bespeaks a great deal of Katie's carrying on the family traditions found in so many of the city's neighborhood dining establishments.

Truth be told, there's not a lot of innovation to be found on the menu at Katie's. It's the type of food people expect in a New Orleans neighborhood restaurant: the usual array of appetizers, salads, sandwiches, plate lunches that lean toward the Italian, sides and desserts. They offer a dozen different pizzas and a daily special as well. There's also a fairly predictable Sunday brunch containing a half-dozen tarted-up egg dishes and New Orleans standards like grillades with grits, crawfish beignets and pain perdu, but also offering the genial amenity of endless Bloody Marys, sangria or mimosas. All in all, it's a very straightforward menu, despite an unfortunate inclination toward bewilderingly non-descriptive or cutesy-poo names that reflect not so much the food, but rather the hapless copywriter's halfway successful capacity for wit.

The reasons for Katie's post-Katrina success and snowballing reputation are the cooking itself and a sharp eye for the details that lift the entire restaurant experience another level or two. A telling example of this came from The Sensible One's never-ending quest for the best onion rings in the entire New Orleans area (Current Leader in the Clubhouse according to TSI: Mandina's). Listed on the menu as "Over-the-Top Onion Rings" because of their relatively vertical presentation (groan), the rings themselves are among the city's more successful versions of the wider, more heavily battered variety. What helps give the rings their "lift" is placing them on a nickel's worth of spring greens and maybe another penny's worth of what appeared to be Tony Chachere's Original Creole Seasoning sprinkled around the rim of the plate.

Another nice idea not commonly seen in the area was "The Crabby Couple," described by their recidivistic copywriter as "two soft shell crabs living a happy life together on two pistolettes" (I'm not making this up). Essentially, it's two small poor boys, an idea that makes increasing sense with every consumed appetizer. Served with Zapp's chips on the side, they are presented in a sturdy and colorful wicker basket instead of the red plastic cheapies found in most poor boy places that serve their sandwiches in something more than rolled butcher paper.

Katie's is quirky enough that it has been descended upon by Guy Fieri of Diners, Drive-Ins & Dives, but the only real remainder of his visit is an oversized poster of the spiky-haired host. In that sense, Katie's has fared better than many Fieri-visited restaurants by keeping its eye on the ball and resisting the temptation to become a gaudy shrine to the TV host, a ghastly example of which is best found at a place with the charming name Louis and the Redhead Lady.

For the record, Fieri sampled "The Boudreaux," a pizza featuring cochon du lait, roasted garlic, fresh spinach, red onion, scallions, and a roasted garlic butter cream reduction. It was a wise choice. Over numerous visits, it has become one of our favorite pizzas in the city, along with "The Terranova," which features home-ground sausage from the Terranova Brothers Superette, a three-aisle corner grocery less than a mile away.

During his visit, Fieri also sampled "The Barge" perhaps the city's ultimate over-the-top poor boy consisting of an entire thirty-two inch Gendusa French loaf overstuffed with fried shrimp, catfish and oysters, fully dressed and serving two to four people. While I have never sampled one, I've seen them come out of the kitchen, and they really make me think "Oh my God" instead of "Wow," more or less how I feel about Fieri's televised clowning.

While food is definitely the driving force behind the renewed success of Katie's, first-rate cooking is not all that rare a commodity in New Orleans. Nor is it all that difficult to find restaurants owned and operated by a nuclear family for their extended "families." What is unusual, however, is to find both components of success so brilliantly in balance and having the whole enterprise enhanced by the attention to small details that normally separate restaurants with white tablecloths from those whose are covered in red gingham.

Katie's appears on the surface to combine all three of those components of success with equal aplomb from the perspective of a chair at one of the restaurant's tables. But anyone who has ever stood on the bank of a still pond and watched a swan effortlessly glide across the water knows that more goes on beneath the surface than ever meets the eye.

Instead of belonging in a better neighborhood, Katie's makes Mid-City a better neighborhood in which to belong.

Katie's Restaurant & Bar
Neighborhood Dining
3701 Iberville Street (at North Telemachus Streets)
Lunch through dinner, Tuesday – Saturday
Lunch only Monday, Sunday brunch
Accepts major credit cards, no reservations
Telephone: (504) 488-6582
Website: www.katiesinmidcity.com

Parkway Bakery & Tavern

For those with larger appetites (and a handy change of clothes), Parkway offers its own Surf N'Turf, a combination of roast beef, gravy and fried shrimp.

Considering the number of dishes created in Crescent City kitchens, it may be an exercise in futility to single out one as the city's definitive dish.

A legitimate case could be made for gumbo, even though its bona fide origins are shrouded in the mists of history. Epicures of a more contemporary stripe have been known to advocate Paul Prudhommes's game-changing blackened redfish. There's a Monday ritual so historically woven into the New Orleans' culinary fabric that the city's all-time favorite son, Louis Armstrong, always closed his letters with, "Red Beans and Rice-ly." Some may point out Oysters Rockefeller or the city's buttery "barbecue" shrimp, and I have little doubt that Bananas Foster has its own sweet-toothed cheering section as well.

Allow me, however, to champion the food that is served in more places and consumed by more people with greater regularity than any of the redoubtable choices cited above. I refer, of course, to the humble "poor boy," New Orleans' swaggering answer to the hoagie, the hero, the grinder or submarine sandwich.

In a city where arguing about food is part of the collective DNA, people not only lock horns about what constitutes the perfect poor boy or who makes it, they can't even reach a consensus on what to call the damned thing. It's a "po-tay-to, po-tah-to" squabble to be sure, with some headstrong natives vehemently calling the sandwich a "poor boy" while others emphatically insist that it's a "po-boy."

While a brief history of the sandwich may never resolve the

nomenclature dispute, it can prove instructive just the same.

In 1929, New Orleanians for the most part went to work on a network of electrified streetcars and both sides of the river were connected by a series of ferries. The public transportation upon which the city was so reliant was plunged into turmoil by a strike that would keep streetcar workers off their rails for four months. Lacking much of a social safety net, hunger for the striking workers was anything but abstract.

Enter Clovis Martin who, along with his brother Bennie, had been a streetcar conductor before opening Martin Brothers Coffee Stand & Restaurant, and whose feelings of solidarity wouldn't allow him to watch his former brethren starve. In a gesture of civic munificence, he offered free sandwiches to striking workers. As workers started showing up at the café, Martin's workers would joke, "here comes another poor boy," and the name soon stuck to the sandwiches.

It didn't take long before "poor boy" was bastardized to "po-boy," which more closely echoes the local pronunciation once it's ground down to patois. Since dyed-in-the-wool New Orleanians will squabble over culinary nomenclature as gamely as they debate the integrity of ingredients, it took no time for "poor boy vs. po-boy" to become the basis for a dispute, and this never-ending quarrel has now raged into its 86th year.

In the past few years, the battle has been joined by local restaurant blogger Tom Fitzmorris and Errol Laborde, the curmudgeonly editor of New Orleans Magazine, both of whom can become quite vociferous about the history and heritage of the humble sandwich and the ensuing moral obligation to use the moniker more accurately reflective of its origin. Out of deference to my more literary brethren, I have chosen to follow their lead and use "poor boy" except in instances where the other spelling is used in a name, title or quotation.

Of course, arguments about poor boys aren't limited to their spelling. In fact, about the only notion to achieve consensus is, "If it isn't on French bread, it really isn't a poor boy." This is despite the fact that, in a classic example of true New Orleans logic, the two most commonly used breads come from bakeries with names that are German

(Leidenheimer) and Italian (Gambino). Of course, the superiority of each nationality's products is the source for a continuing dispute in and of itself.

The poor boy loaf as it is baked today was actually developed for the Martin Brothers by local baker John Gendusa. The Martins specified an elongated French loaf, 32 inches in length, with the classic baguette ends to be non-tapered for easier slicing and less waste. While every bakery has its own techniques that it claims superior, the 32-inch loaf as engineered by Gendusa in 1929 remains the standard.

Naturally, with the innate versatility coming from the fact that the poor boy is first and foremost a sandwich, for Pete's sake, it only follows that there's no agreement on the best ingredients to put between those French loaves produced by Italian and German bakeries. To that end, Parkway Bakery & Tavern offers 25 different poor boys, while Johnny's Po'Boys in the French Quarter weighs in with a staggering 46. While it isn't uncommon to find such eccentric variations as a French fry and gravy poor boy, fried calamari or one that's filled with stewed duck, the two varieties most commonly seen across the Crescent City are fried shellfish and gravy drenched roast beef.

It is generally acknowledged that the first poor boy was indeed roast beef, for which the brothers Martin charged a princely fifteen cents (at least to everyone except their striking comrades).

New Orleans roast beef is slow-cooked in a gravy that's thicker than that generally found in Chicago Italian beef or French dip sandwiches. Once "dressed," New Orleans vernacular for lettuce, tomatoes and mayonnaise (pronounced "my-nez" locally) with pickles, onions and Zatarain's Creole mustard optional, there is usually little way to contain all the ingredients in the flaky crust and airy-centered poor boy loaf in which the conglomeration is assembled. Oh, hell, let's just call it what it is; it's a mess, albeit a glorious one.

In 2012, Brett Anderson, the highly regarded restaurant critic for The Times-Picayune, went on a months-long quest to determine the city's premier roast beef poor boy, during which time he tried ever gravy-dripping poor boy recommended to him by the newspaper's readers. After sampling over sixty sandwiches and writing reviews of nearly two dozen of them, he declared the champ to be R&O's, a Lakeview pizza, plate lunch and poor boy joint. Instead of settling the debate, this only re-ignited it, but what else would you expect in a metropolitan area of roughly 1.2 million people that serves as home to roughly 1.2 million food critics?

And in case you're wondering, yes, fried shellfish poor boys have been known to spark equally heated discussions over the years.

Settling poor boy feuds has now spread far beyond the confines of the Crescent City and into television homes all over America. Iron Chef's Michael Symon, host of The Food Network's short-lived Food Feuds pitted Parkway Bakery & Tavern's roast beef poor boy against that of Tracey's (Parkway won). Rachel Ford's Food Wars staged a fried shrimp poor boy food fight between Parkway and Domilise's, one of the city's oldest bars and sandwich shops (Domilise's won). Man vs. Food's mega-glutton, Adam Richman, declared the Domilise's shrimp poor boy the best sandwich in the American South in his coast-to-coast hunt for the nation's best sandwich. Finally, numerous shops specializing in poor boys have served as the straight man to the lowbrow antics of the ubiquitous Guy Fieri on Diners, Drive-Ins & Dives.

So who has the best poor boy in New Orleans?

Who knows?

I think the only correct answer is, "Whoever you think does."

With all due respect to Brett Anderson of The Times-Picayune, I think the best roast beef poor boy comes from a place with the delightfully prosaic name Sammy's Food Service & Deli. And while Domilise's is certainly one of the city's great joints, the shrimp are bigger, sweeter and somehow seem fresher at Parkway.

That said, people with enough time to explore just one poor boy place on short visits to the city would do well to consider Parkway Bakery and Tavern in the Mid-City area.

Parkway is the very embodiment of old-line New Orleans neighborhood places. An unadorned frame building sitting on a corner in a tattered-but-gentrifying section of the city, it is at once a neighborhood landmark and a wistful reminder of better days both behind and ahead. First opened in 1911, the place had been boarded up before a local entrepreneur restored and reopened it in the early 2000s before it had to be redone a second time in Katrina's aftermath.

There is an essential honesty about Parkway that "is what it is" without pretense or affectation. The front room is a small bar, the back room a utilitarian sandwich café, and outside there is a covered deck and patio, where bands sometimes play on weekends or the spontaneous, informal holidays that seem so often to spring up on the New Orleans calendar. The decor is mainly old signs and pieces of Saints memorabilia.

The sandwiches come to your table or barstool wrapped in white butcher paper. Napkins are in a dispenser along with salt, pepper and New Orleans-made Crystal Hot Sauce wrapped in a Parkway label. The wait staff is young and cheerful.

As mentioned above, Parkway's menu lists twenty-five poor boys in either regular (eight-inch) or large (twelve-inch) sizes. A good many of them are traditional and predictable (ham, turkey, marinara meatball, chicken breast, various sausages and the like).

Because of New Orleans' gulf location, fresh seafood is abundant, making fried shrimp and oyster poor boys the other main entries in the Parkway repertoire. During their short season, the restaurant occasionally lists soft shell crab poor boys as blackboard specials. For those with larger appetites (and a handy change of clothes), Parkway offers its own Surf N'Turf, a combination of roast beef, gravy and fried shrimp.

Beyond the traditional standards, Parkway has a gravy only poor boy on the menu, as well as one made with French fried potatoes where one would expect to find meat. This has progressed, of course, into the fully dressed, gravy-slathered, French fries poor boy. In a nod to Louisiana's Cajun heritage, the restaurant also lists an alligator sausage poor boy on its lengthy menu.

While Parkway has full bar service, a look at the tables will show most of them covered with frosty beer bottles or longnecks of Barq's root beer, a regional favorite long before it was purchased by the Coca-Cola

Company, and the traditional accompaniment for a classic New Orleans poor boy.

Because of its informality, Parkway is a good place to bring the kids, as evidenced by the fact the when visiting New Orleans on the fifth anniversary of Katrina, President Obama brought Michele and the girls there for lunch. For the record, the girls had burgers, the President and Mrs. O had shrimp poor boys, before the President forgot to take the carry-out dessert (banana pudding) he purchased back to Air Force One.

My advice, should you choose to drop in on Parkway, is to follow the presidential lead and order the shrimp poor boy instead of the roast beef. The roast beef poor boy is perfectly satisfactory, of course, but not out-of-the-park outstanding; in truth, it's fairly average as far as New Orleans poor boys are concerned. The shrimp, on the other hand, truly rises above what I've tasted in other poor boy joints around the city, and when given a choice between exceptional and average, well, duh.

Parkway Bakery and Tavern
Poor Boys
539 Hagan Avenue (at the corner of Toulouse).
Lunch through dinner, Wednesday through Monday
All major credit cards are accepted.
Telephone: (504) 482-3047
Website: www.parkwaypoorboys.com

R&O's

Perhaps the best way to describe the extensive menu is "Round up the usual suspects".

I'm not one who cheerfully stands in line. Cooling my heels in line for a table doesn't raise my expectations, only my blood pressure. Even at my favorite New Orleans restaurant, Galatoire's, when I see the line extend more than twenty-five feet from the front door, I vamoose.

Consequently, the first time I entered the wraparound entryway of R&O's in the Bucktown neighborhood, the sight of fifteen benches and a dozen stray chairs ready to accommodate fifty-some customers far more patient than me made for an ominous start. Fortunately, with her unfathomable forbearance of my hair-trigger curmudgeonliness, The Sensible One gently pointed out that the restaurant had just opened for the day and there remained a few tables as empty as the foyer benches.

Truth told, any waiting area one-third the size of the restaurant within often means one of three things:

1. The proprietor is a cockeyed optimist.

2. The owner is hoping that the large waiting area will give the impression of a huge demand for seating and thereby generate a snowball effect.

3. The place is really that good.

R&O's is that good.

Trying to put a finger on my basis for such a conclusion, I can't come up with one single reason. Rather, I think R&O's is one of those cases where, to trot out that dreadful cliché, the whole is greater than the sum of its parts.

Despite only dating back to 1980, R&O's is a latter-day continuation of the New Orleans tradition of opening as another kind of business before becoming a restaurant. Parkway, one of the city's premier poor boy shops, began life as a Mid-City bakery. Mandina's, considered by many the city's definitive neighborhood restaurant, started selling sandwiches when it was a pool hall. The legendary Mosca's evolved from a swamp-side roadhouse named Wildwood Tavern. R&O's, the subject at hand, started in the tiny back room of a ramshackle grocery store.

A true Mom & Pop operation, R&O's (so dubbed for founders Roland and Ora) expanded into first a pizza parlor before expanding once again into its current incarnation of poor boy, platter and pizza emporium. While many, if not most, restaurants seem to lose momentum in proportion to expansion, that isn't the case at R&O's, which seems to have expanded its customer base even more rapidly than its real estate.

For the type of place it is, R&O's is relatively large with a capacity in the neighborhood of 150 people. When the restaurant is full, and it often is, the members of the wait staff have to carefully maneuver trays between the tables, improvising and then navigating impossibly narrow walkways. The attendant noise level puts R&O high on the list of restaurants you'd be least likely to select for a romantic meal, but that's not the point of the place anyway.

Ultimately, R&O's is not a place to "dine" in the most elegant sense of the word. Rather, it seems to be the first place anyone on the west suburban part of the city thinks of when someone says, "Let's go get something to eat."

The room is as Saturday afternoon casual as the dress code. Multicolored Christmas tree lights line the inside rafters. No matter where you sit, you'll be sure to see a poster, banner, newspaper front page, brewery sign or knickknack celebrating the city's beloved NFL Saints. Despite food that can sometimes prove messy to eat, there are no napkins provided, or napkin holders on the tables, but instead rolls of paper towels on vertical stands serve that utilitarian purpose.

As one might expect in a place that clearly caters to a local, middle class clientele, the servers, mostly middle-aged women, somehow manage to keep smiles on their faces while ceaselessly hustling an army's worth of food through tight spaces to ravenous hordes. Despite the fact that I find myself older than the majority of them, the way they coddle and cluck over me whisks me back a half-century to suppertime at Mom's kitchen table.

The drawing card at R&O's is the food, period, and there is nothing fancy, pretentious or precious about it. It is straightforward New Orleans casual with a Sicilian "red gravy" accent. Perhaps the best way to describe the extensive menu is "Round up the usual suspects". Consider:

• The menu lists eighteen appetizers ranging from seasonal boiled shellfish to French fries smothered in gravy

• There are three soups and a half dozen salads

• Twenty-five sandwiches are listed before add-ons, from the ubiquitous muffuletta to soft-shell crab Parmesan served on sesame-seeded Italian rolls instead of the more traditional poor boy loaf

• Eight mostly Italian specials are offered at weekday lunch

• Thin or thick crust pizzas, both hand-tossed, are available with a choice of twenty toppings

• The twenty-four dinner choices are mainly seafood, Sicilian or a traditional hybrid of the two

• A true, kid-friendly family place, R&O's offers nine children's plates of real food (with not a hot dog, hamburger or chicken tender in sight).

Even by New Orleans standards, the portions are generous. Plus, for the underfed itinerant lumberjack or the garden-variety masochist, there are three desserts on the menu and usually a couple of chalkboard suggestions.

The cooking is not imaginative, but workmanlike, and that may be the true secret of R&O's continuing success. Of course, it didn't hurt matters when The Times-Picayune restaurant critic pronounced their roast beef poor boy the city's hands-down best after a six-month search.

Even in New Orleans, a city where kitchens seem to be abandoning homegrown traditional cuisine in favor of the trickiest post-hip trend and so-called (and often self-styled) celebrity/superstar chefs are sprouting up like so much culinary crabgrass, the number of people deriving comfort from the familiar far exceeds the vocal minority of fad chasers. While I do not have the statistics at hand, I would be willing to wager that during R&O's 34-year run of dishing up dependability, it's far more likely that the number of gimmick-chasing eateries that have opened and shuttered their doors can be more easily counted by the hundred than the dozen.

In all candor, were I able to have time for only one meal on a trip to New Orleans, it would more likely be at a place that's more upscale than R&O's. There are, after all, any number of restaurants in New Orleans where the cooking is more heroic, the servers more polished and the surroundings more genteel.

That said, there remains a school of thought suggesting that if you want to learn what the city it truly all about, the farther you get away from the established tourism and convention districts, the closer to its heart you'll get.

You may very well take exception to such a statement, and that's more than okay, but I know of a place where more than fifty people with growling stomachs patiently sit on wooden benches waiting to disagree.

R&O's

Poor boys, Platters & Pizza

216 Old Hammond Highway in Metairie

Lunch, daily

Dinner, Wednesday - Sunday

Credit cards honored

No reservations

Telephone (501) 831-1248

No website

LOCAL COLOR

Because New Orleans itself often defies categorization, it should come as no surprise that some of its more interesting restaurants don't fit into people's expectations of the city.

For decades, New Orleans has been most famous for elegant, gracious restaurants offering haute Creole cuisines, and should you ask most travelers to name the city's restaurants, the old standbys like Galatoire's and Antoine's would turn up toward the top of the list.

Like all cities, however, New Orleans keeps evolving, sometimes for the better, sometimes not. Starting roughly forty years ago, the more rural Cajun methods of food preparation started having a pronounced influence on the city's cuisine. The proliferation of cooking television programs, websites and magazines have added more flavors to all American cuisine, and New Orleans, despite its traditionally hidebound feelings about what constitutes proper cooking, has not been exempted.

If there is anything of a constant left in New Orleans beyond change itself, it's the eccentric attitudes of the city's people, as much a melting pot amalgam as the Crescent City's signature dish, gumbo. New Orleanians, like people anywhere, have been forced to adapt to change, but unlike other people anywhere, they do it reluctantly, begrudgingly and not very well.

This final section of five definitive city restaurants looks at five establishments and how they have adapted to changing tastes, changing demographics and a changing world. Some have done it with aplomb, like an old steakhouse that found new life after Hurrican Katrina and a greasy spoon that changed with élan when the city's oldest neighborhood came out of the closet.

There's the story of a start-up seafood place in a blue-collar neighborhood that was forced to build its reputation on roast beef when Katrina decimated the city's seafood industry. And there's a look at a throwback boiled crawfish café that has changed perhaps less than any other I have come across during my forty-year love affair with the city.

The final restaurant, the city's second oldest, is trying to renew its foothold in three different centuries and the results have been mixed at best.

In this cantankerous city, where people argue about every ingredient, cooking technique, restaurant menu, chef and anything else they can think to quibble about, they also argue about change itself and when a beloved establishment changes, the jury will be forever out.

Charlie's Steak House

That said, Charlie's still exudes a raffish charm,
starting with its menu or, to be more precise, lack of one.

It took Charlie's Steak House three years to re-open after Hurricane Katrina, during which time The Sensible One and I would check monthly to see if there was any word.

Before the storm, Charlie's had been a tattered, down-at-the-heels neighborhood place featuring okay food served with a cranky attitude. It was cheap and we were living paycheck-to-paycheck, so there was a certain symbiosis to the arrangement.

When word got out that Charlie's had reopened, we were over-joyed. We went, and we were disappointed.

Maybe our palates had become more sophisticated, or it could have been that our wallets had gained a little weight and we had started patronizing pricier places with better grades of steak.

Or it could have been that compared to the old dump, the new place had been spiffed up a little and was beginning to border on being the kind of restaurant to which I could take people I wanted to entertain, rather than unnerve.

After reconsidering it a little, however, I feel comfortable suggesting it to friends, albeit guardedly.

As an aficionado of tattered, threadbare places that surprise with good chow, then delight with reasonable checks, I am prone to outbursts of nostalgia, particularly when acts get cleaned up. To me, Cinderella was far more interesting as a beleaguered stepsister than a glass-slippered princess, the sudden prince was never as riveting as the cursed frog and in that vein Charlie's was more enticing ramshackle than respectable.

That said, Charlie's still exudes a raffish charm, starting with its menu or, to be more precise, lack of one. Before Katrina, once you were seated, your server would snarl something along the lines of, "Whaddya want?" Upon realizing that you were a hopeless rookie, he or she would bark out, "We got the little T-bone, the big T-bone, the Charlie and we got the filet, so whaddya want?"

You were expected to know that the Charlie is a 32 oz. T-bone that drips over the side of the plate as well as what side dishes they offer, so who needs a menu? You say you do? "It's been da same since Mr. Charlie Petrossi opened da door in 1932, so where've you been?" The gruffness, of course, was part of the tradition and on occasion not sincere, but it served to tell you that you weren't in a snooty place so you better not act like it.

In the newer incarnation of Charlie's the grumpy fishwives who once ruled the floor have been traded in for a corps of attentive, youngish gentlemen who serve customers with more finesse than fireworks. It may be service with a smile instead of a snarl these days, but I always felt that being treated like an unwelcome in-law was part of the joint's charm, a backhanded lagniappe that not only made me feel at home, but also heralded straightforward, no-frills, rock-solid cooking.

Regarding the sides (and there are six of them), they are as old school steakhouse as everything else about the place — onion rings, potatoes au gratin, steak fries, salad, sautéed mushrooms and garlic bread. They are so good and the portions are so enormous I've started working on this idea that one night, I could pretend to be a vegetarian and only order side dishes, hoping they don't toss me out onto Dryades Street.

Very few New Orleanians would dispute the primacy of Charlie's onion rings in the city and quite possibly far beyond. The salad greens are basic, B-flat iceberg lettuce, but they come engulfed in a blue cheese dressing blended with enough garlic to keep Italy operating for a month or two. The garlic bread is made the time-honored Italian way — buttered, studded with garlic cloves and broiled. Having gorged myself with onion rings, salad, and bread every time I visit, I have yet to get around to the potatoes or mushrooms.

While the notion of going to a steakhouse for the sides instead of the main event may be unusual, it actually makes some kind of paradoxical sense at Charlie's, because, in fact, the sides are better than the steaks. That's not to say there's anything inherently bad about the steaks, but it doesn't take more than a bite or two to realize that the beef being served isn't USDA Prime (or if it is, someone might want to think of standing the chef in front of a firing squad).

The steaks are most likely USDA Choice, generally on par with what is sold in a better neighborhood supermarket. It's very good meat, but it's just not up to the level of the top two percent (Prime), which is sold in so many "big boy" or "A" steakhouses in major American cities these days. But to Charlie's everlasting credit, they don't charge big boy prices for what they proudly put on the plate.

The crux of the story is that the quality grade of the beef is what keeps Charlie's from becoming one of the small circle of elite steakhouses in a city that isn't as well known for very good steak as it might be. But a major part of the true beauty of the place is that it doesn't pretend to be what it isn't.

In recent years, Charlie's has added a rib eye and a strip to its steak offerings, but beyond that not much has changed except the prices and with any luck at all, not much ever will. The truth is, Charlie's is a straightforward neighborhood steakhouse that serves a good steak dinner for a good steak price, and its lack of artifice may very well be one of the key reasons it's been a going concern for nearly eighty years.

Consider the exceptional sides and occasionally still being treated like an in-law as added bonuses.

Charlie's Steak House
Steaks & Sides
4510 Dryades (between Napoleon Avenue and Valence Street)
Dinner, Tuesday - Saturday
Reservations are suggested
Major credit cards honored
Telephone: (504) 895-9323
Website: www.charliessteakhousenola.com

Clover Grill

If you happen to be sitting at the counter and watching the cook work,
you might even feel your arteries clog up right on the spot.

May you relish my what?

"May we relish your weenie?" There it was, right on the menu of the Clover Grill under the "Clover Weenie." Even though the revised menu no longer carries that, uh, proposition, the high camp iconoclasm of the Clover remains in full flower 24/7.

An openly gay greasy spoon where burgers are grilled under hubcaps, eggs are scrambled in a milkshake blender and you expect the fryboys to break into dance at the drop of a counterman's paper cap, the Clover is the first café you'll bump into on Bourbon Street once you cross New Orleans' "Lavender Line."

Even though the signs may read St. Ann Street, the so-called Lavender Line is the unofficial border separating the bustling commercial section of the French Quarter from its quieter, more residential area with its high concentration of gay residents. Within the lower quarter is a two square-block area known as "The Fruit Loop," which is the self-described epicenter of the city's gay nightlife, attractions, and events.

The Clover Grill's location on "the Loop" shares the corner of Bourbon and Dumaine with Café Lafitte in Exile, one of the oldest gay bars in the country. One block further down Bourbon Street is Jean Lafitte's Blacksmith Shop, a picturesque pile of a tavern built circa 1772 and reputed to be the oldest continuously operated saloon in the United States. Go another block and you'll be at an all-night grocery named the QuarterMaster, but generally referred to locally as the "Nellie Deli."

The bottom line is that the neighborhood is sure to make the hardest-bitten homophobe roughly as comfortable as a deacon in a cathouse.

Even though there is no question about the sexual identity of the Clover or a seeming majority of its patrons, most of the stereotypical vamping and camping is played for laughs instead of keeps. Just the same, it can be somewhat unnerving to the unsuspecting, sleepy-eyed visitor who wanders in for nothing more than breakfast when an elegantly made-up gentleman working the cash register breaks into a bumping, grinding lip-sync to The Weather Girls' rendition of It's Raining Men (Hallelujah) cascading out of the jukebox.

The Clover is a tiny place — only eleven red-topped stools at the split counter and four tables. What's more, it's visually bland. The white-washed exterior probably hasn't changed much since 1939, the year generally thought to be when the diner opened although no one is sure enough to bet a dollar on it. There's a fading generic Coca-Cola sign at the corner and the dining room is awash in pink tile. A sign painted on the window proclaims "HAMBURGERS WORLD'S BEST." If it hadn't been plopped down in the middle of Bourbon Street, it could be anywhere else in America.

The menu is generic — a build-your-own burger, a short order breakfast, chicken fried steak, a pork chop, waffle, omelets, some predictable sandwiches and, of course, the Clover Weenie. Scattered through the menu are about a dozen quips, the humor value of which generally falls somewhere between a groaner and out-and-out lame. "We don't eat in your bed, so please don't sleep at our table. Our chili speaks for itself...sooner or later. You can beat our prices, but you can't beat our meat." The only thing missing is a septuagenarian drummer firing off vaudeville rimshots.

It is tempting to say that the key to the Clover's success is that everything is served with a side order of attitude, but that would be inaccurate because, really, attitude is the main course. Without its sassy, brassy attitude, the Clover would be just another overlooked diner with a New Orleans address. That would be a shame, too, because the food is surprisingly good for its category.

That's not to say the food is a beautifully styled work of art when it arrives. Chances are it was slopped on a homely ceramic plate that landed at your place at the counter or table with a brusque thump. While the service is both affable and thoughtful, not to mention funny as hell at times, it isn't graceful. It will be a long time, perhaps one afternoon when there are snowball fights in Jackson Square, before any of them trade in their Clover t-shirts for tuxedos and start tossing out bon mots in French at Antoine's.

The food itself makes me think of the point in time, most likely in college, when I discovered that breakfast was more than fuel to be bolted down before dashing off to a snooze-worthy lecture. It's late night, after midnight chow, designed to soak up excess booze without making someone want another round. This is acknowledged on the Clover's website, where a mini-ad reads, "We're Open 24 Hours Because Food Tastes Better After Midnight."

The active ingredient at breakfast appears to be butter, enough butter to make a cardiologist start counting new money or TV chef Paula Deen to be overcome with a case of the vapors. In fact, sitting on the edge of the flat-top is a tall saucepot of melted butter, into which a ladle is regularly dipped and its contents poured over eggs and grits. If you happen to be sitting at the counter watching the cook work, you might even feel your arteries seize up right on the spot.

The scrambled eggs and omelets are remarkably light and fluffy, the result of being spun with a splash of icy water in an old soda parlor milkshake blender. Eggs are fried directly on the flat-top before being (surprise!) finished with butter.

There is the general assortment of meats one expects in a short order joint. Having developed a personal aversion to breakfast bacon being cooked to the point it can be snapped with my fingers, I unthinkingly told the waiter that I wanted my meat limp. Suffice it to say that the ensuing cackling and pandemonium on the part of the kitchen staff reminded me that the Clover might not have been the wisest place to make such a request.

The gimmick of hamburgers at the Clover Grill is that when

they're sizzling on the flat-top, they're covered with a hubcap (always American-made, so they claim), which serves to steam the beef patty while it cooks. What results is a juicy, home-style burger with a home-made flavor, something that seems more difficult to find nowadays, when more and more restaurants cook on open grills or in broilers, and short order cafés have been replaced by fast food emporia. To loyal Clover patrons, their hubcap burger proudly serves as a defiant refutation of food writer Calvin Trillin's tenet that "anybody who doesn't think that the best hamburger place in the world is in his home town is a sissy."

In a place where waiters proudly sport ball caps emblazoned with "DIVA" and "Delta Queen," where hard-earned hangovers are nursed with strong coffee and unsuspecting tourists drop their jaws at the 24/7 floor show, the quality of the food is often overlooked. To do so at the Clover Grill would be a grave injustice. It may not be ambitious, trendy or urbane, but thank God it doesn't try to be. The Clover dishes up straight-ahead, classic American hash house chow without apology, be-cause with solid, filling food prepared this well, apologies become need-less.

Of course, the place has its detractors. The Clover is totally po-larizing; people may love it or loathe it, but chances are they'll never forget it. And through it all, the cooks and countermen just keep on dancing. Hallelujah.

The Clover Grill
Diner
900 Bourbon Street (at Dumaine)
Open 24/7 with no reservations
Credit cards accepted
Telephone: (504) 598-1010
Website: www.clovergrill.com

Sal's Seafood

Keep eating and wadding up paper napkins until the tabletop resembles
the aftermath of a pitched battle.

If boiled crawfish didn't taste so good, I'd probably think their only reason for being would be to intimidate diners encountering the little critters for the very first time. I certainly remember losing my "Louisiana lobster" virginity. What's more, I suspect most people who didn't grow up in the southern parts of Louisiana also have their initial "man vs. mudbug" moment somewhere in their memory banks.

Mine came in a metal oilfield equipment shed on the highway joining Lafayette and New Iberia. I was in the heart of Cajun country to work as a celebrity handler on an institutional video shoot and, after four days on location, the client wanted to throw a wrap party for our noted Hollywood actor, the late Arthur Hill, and the production crew. It was a lovely gesture on the part of the client, and Arthur, a soft-spoken gentleman who was as shy in person as he could be commanding on screen, reluctantly agreed.

When we showed up at the shed, a genuine Cajun fais do-do was in full swing. Beer kegs were doing land office business. Some of the warehouse workers and roughnecks had formed a pick-up band and enthusiastic if not virtuoso zydeco music was reverberating off the metal building's walls. People were dancing and keeping an eye on a large aluminum cooker over a propane flame waiting for the pot to come to a rolling boil. Off to the side was a galvanized horse trough, in which thousands of live, greenish crawfish wriggled and crawled on top of each other.

Arthur took one look into the trough and glanced at me with a pained expression that asked what the hell was I getting him into. I didn't know what to tell him; I had eaten plenty of peeled crawfish tails since coming to the South, but had never encountered one still encased in its shell. The Cajun in charge of the whole shebang was opening several boxes of iodized salt and asked the actor if he had ever been to a crawfish boil. Arthur said he indeed hadn't. Starting to pour the salt on the teeming crawfish in order to purge them, the Cajun cheerfully said, "The first thing we do is to get them to spit up all the crap in their guts."

Once Arthur's natural color returned to his face and the crawfish were boiled to their characteristic crimson or red-orange, it was time to learn how to "shuck and suck."

There is a technique to eating crawfish in southern Louisiana that isn't as difficult as it seems when someone first encounters a steaming pile of what the natives call "mudbugs" if they're feeling particularly formal or just plain "bugs" when they're not. The first step is to break the crawfish in half at the joint where its head/abdomen meets the tail.

The next step is to suck the yellowish fat and peppery juice out of the broken end of the head/abdomen, because that's where the richest flavor is found. And yes, more people than not are squeamish, appalled, self-conscious and feel like they look like idiots (which they do) the first time when and if they reluctantly give it a try.

The tail half of the crawfish is far less daunting. Grab the meat protruding out the end where it was joined to the head, pinch the spot on the tail where the shell-shaped fin is connected and pull. It will easily extract the meat from the shell. Pop it in your mouth and that's it. Suck the head, pinch the tail, and enjoy the flavor most people will say is halfway between that of a shrimp and a lobster.

Arthur never quite got the hang of the procedure, but he didn't have to. On either side of him were a couple of Cajun women who were all too happy to peel the tails for a film and television personality (and he wasn't about to suck the head). Me, it took about a half dozen false starts and it all became so natural I briefly considered changing my name to Boudreaux.

In the years since, I've enjoyed crawfish during its seasons (roughly late December through early June, weather depending) in saloons, joints, dumps and eateries from one end of the New Orleans metropolitan area to the other. Almost every place I had them became my new favorite, that is until I found Sal's Seafood, a thoroughly unprepossessing café in Marrero, one of the bedroom communities dotting the West Bank (which in New Orleans is actually east of the East Bank).

Sal's is in a thoroughly nondescript building you'd drive right past were it not emblazoned with a building-wide sign touting HOT BOILED FRESH LIVE SEAFOOD OYSTER BAR. The parking lot is gravel. There's an open area behind the building where the boilers are, and one look tells you there's enough equipment to boil shrimp, crabs or crawfish for several hundred people at once.

Inside, the place has all the ambience and charm of the employee lunchroom in a rundown factory. The walls are white and mostly blank. The furniture is utilitarian and it's pretty apparent it was bought for price instead of customer comfort. At the end of the bar in the back corner of the room is a tall stack of newspapers. Through a door in the back of the room is a small take-out seafood market. The scattered tables are occupied by working folks from nearby and it's obvious they've known each other for decades.

The menu is basic. Boiled seafood, poor boy sandwiched and sides are joined by a couple of fried platters and dinner plates of either red or white beans and rice. From time to time, there'll be a special or two on the blackboard.

What I like most about Sal's is its authenticity. Once TS1 and I decide how many pounds of crawfish we're going to have, the woman who takes our order drifts over to the bar, grabs a handful of newspaper sections and spreads them across our linoleum-topped table on her return.

After a few minutes, she comes back carrying a brown paper bag, out of which she pours our order of crawfish, still steaming from the boiler, on the spread out newspaper. Beer and soft drinks are in ice-cold cans and glasses or plastic cups are no place to be seen.

The drill is simple. Eat the crawfish with your fingers and dump the shells wherever you can find a place on the newspaper "tablecloth." Drink the Budweiser out of the can. Keep eating and wadding up paper napkins until the tabletop resembles the aftermath of a pitched battle. Figure where in the world the woman will find space to dump the two more pounds of crawfish you wouldn't have ordered until you found out they were even better than you remembered them being the last time.

Sal's may be the last place in the New Orleans area where a paper sack of steaming bugs is dumped onto a pile of newspaper. These days, most places seem to serve them on round plastic advertising trays from breweries and the beer all too often shows up in a chilled mug. I'm sorry, but it's just not the same.

To put a fine point on it, Sal's is the real deal, the genuine article, and maybe it's the last of its breed. I hope it's around and doesn't change, at least until I'm finished bouncing around on this planet. It's far too good, and far too real, to ever be consigned to the scrap heap of memory.

Every time I go into Sal's I think of Arthur, who sadly passed on before I could drag him in and tell the server, "Bring us a brown paper bag of bugs and keep 'em coming 'til my buddy sucks so many heads and pinches so much tail that he hollers, 'Uncle.'" Some memories, even those of events that never happened, are just too strong to fade.

Sal's Seafood
Local Seafood
1512 Barataria Boulevard, Marrero
Lunch and Dinner, Tuesday - Saturday
Credit Cards honored
No reservations
Telephone: (504) 341-8112
No website

Seither's Seafood

It's smallish, around a dozen tables, a size that seems to be a forerunner of good chow to come in New Orleans.

If, as it has been said, confession is good for the soul, let me do my scruffy soul a little good.

I have always had a soft spot (not to be confused with my often soft head) for places that can politely be called "shacks," when not being less graciously called "dumps."

Surely you know the type of place I'm talking about. You're driving down a back street that's totally new to you, when you see a semiramshackle joint and drive right on by, even as you comment to your companion, "Gee, I bet they dish up some pretty good chow in there." When or if you stop, you take a chance, and the odds are roughly 50-50 the meal will either be awful or border on the divine. Sometimes the food ends up being right in the middle, sure, but when the place is enough of a dive, you're either going to vote it up or down.

The greater New Orleans area is covered up with mid- to downscale dives, but one I happened across when lost and looking for someplace else has become more of a favorite with every visit. Seither's Seafood has only been around since 2004, making it a relative pup in a city where it seems that most restaurants of its ilk are at least a half-century old and on their second, third or higher generation of family ownership. One look at the building tells you it either had a couple of previous business incarnations or a singularly hard decade.

Seither's is hidden away in suburban Harahan, a bedroom community with an apparent case of multiple personality disorder not terribly far from the Huey P. Long Bridge. Parts of Harahan are white collar, housing legions of sales representatives and other types whose lives are bettered by proximity to nearby Louis Armstrong International Airport, but the township is mostly middle-class leaning toward blue collar. The combination restaurant and oyster bar is located on Hickory Avenue, a desultory strip of small, nondescript businesses for which high-visibility locations or heavy traffic counts are of seemingly little consequence.

The joint is quintessentially Crescent City. Before opening the place, its proprietor, Jason Seither, sold cars for a spell and worked as a bartender in a restaurant and fish market in the next suburb. His name-sake restaurant has made as much of its solid reputation through roast beef poor boys as it has for seafood. From all appearances, he's making pretty decent money in a place most people don't know exists and is tough to find for those who do. All this seems to add up to success in "the city that care forgot," where some people stick to the rules, but most seem to make them up as they go along.

Once you walk in the gaudily painted glass door of Seither's, you enter a room that looks exactly like what you'd expect from outside. It's smallish, around a dozen tables, a size that seems to be a harbinger of good chow to come in New Orleans. It's a relatively homely room that leaves no doubt that you have entered perhaps the archetypal mom-and-pop café. The walls are the color of lemon icebox pie, the furniture utilitarian and in place of napkins on the plain tables are rolls of paper towels. A drop ceiling with recessed fluorescents gives the room all the ambient charm of a bail bondsman's office. All of that is, of course, mercifully secondary to the food.

Years ago, roughly around the time Methuselah and I were a pair of rascally schoolboys, any café or restaurant's success or failure was determined entirely by the quality of the food served on the plate. Somewhere in the not too distant past, people stopped simply going to lunch or dinner but rather became participants in "the dining experience." It's my personal theory that the whole "experience" angle was cooked up by marketing hotshots hired by restaurants where the food sucked. At any rate, it's Seither's retrograde and, one suspects dogged, commitment to a laser-like focus on the food that keeps the glass front door swinging open and shut.

The success of Seither's roast beef poor boy is based upon two divergent factors. The first of these was the havoc wreaked upon the city's seafood industry by Hurricane Katrina in 2005. When Seither's re-opened shortly after the storm, shrimp and oysters were nigh on impossible to find and buy. Consequently, the fledgling restaurant was forced to concentrate on the foodstuffs it could actually procure for simple survival.

The second factor was also driven by necessity. While many poor boy shops purchase pre-cooked beef for their sandwiches, Jason Seither was still in his early years struggling for survival and he found that he could buy uncooked sirloin tip roast for less. This he did, slowly cooking it in what he refers to as "crock pot style," a process thought to yield a richer integration of meat and gravy. While self-appointed poor boy purists regularly argue about beef cuts and cooking techniques (a continuing, irresolvable argument no one ever wins), Seither's version of the New Orleans classic quickly developed a loyal following and remains one of the most commonly ordered items to this day.

Perhaps the most unusual thing about the roast beef poor boy's popularity is that the sandwich comes from a restaurant that started life a fresh seafood market before evolving into a small oyster bar several years ago. It's certainly not uncommon for a poor boy joint to be serving both meat and seafood creations, to be sure, but it's somewhat unexpected and perhaps moderately ironic for a restaurant that was once an adjunct to a seafood market to set the cornerstone of its reputation upon a foundation of sirloin tip.

It would be a shortsighted mistake, however, to overlook Seither's seafood poor boys. The shrimp offering overflows with expertly fried shrimp, the taste of which explodes with the unmistakable sweetness of the shellfish when it's freshly caught.

On a recent visit, The Sensible One saw a blackboard special called the "Oysterpalooza" or some equally gimmicky moniker. Essentially it's Seither's take on the "Peacemaker," a combination of fried oysters, bacon and cheddar poor boy so named because it was reputedly proffered to angry wives as a peace offering by husbands staggering in from a hard night of carousing. It was as good as it was big, and the size of it straddled the line between the words "mammoth" and "gargantuan." We could have easily split the silly thing and waddled out of the joint without even thinking about dessert.

Other poor boys that appeared equally intriguing were one featuring a crab cake topped with shrimp sauce, and the shrimp remoulade special the kitchen prepared for the 2010 festival honoring the city's legendary sandwich.

During crawfish season, the heart of which is generally considered to run from Mardi Gras through Memorial Day, parades of beer trays holding piles of steaming mudbugs steadily stream from the kitchen, augmented by traditional corn-on-the-cob and new potatoes. While the bevy of other choices once kept me from sampling a mountain of scorching bugs, I found myself wondering if I'd made a mistake every time I saw or caught a whiff as another tray came of the kitchen. They were reputed to be among the city's best, and I knew the prospect of a steaming pile of them merited a single-digit spot on my personal bucket list. Once I finally ordered a tray of the little critters, my hunch was emphatically realized.

As good as all the sampled chow is and that yet-to-be-sampled promises to be, I'm quite sure that if I brought up the Seither's name in a game of Word Association, The Sensible One would immediately blurt out, "Onion rings!" As much as she considers herself a connoisseur of the deep fried gems, in truth she's more of a fanatic. While the Seither's thick cut and heavily battered entry into her relentless quest for the indisputably best onion ring in the world is the most recent to be awarded the crown, it joins a list that over the years has included "frings" at K-Paul's Louisiana Kitchen, the mountainous servings of thickly sliced rings at Mandina's, Café 615 ("Home of Da Wabbit") on the West Bank, Katie's in Mid-City, a brief nod to the thin-cut rings at Charlie's Steakhouse and even an honorable mention to the deep-fried green pepper rings at Franky and Johnny's Uptown roadhouse. Nonetheless, it remains a ringing endorsement, and one richly deserved.

One of the true joys of learning New Orleans, where joy's pursuit is part of the hardwiring, is coming to terms with the hope that all it takes is making one more turn and you face the very real possibility of stumbling upon a restaurant that's not only good for lunch, it may be one for the ages.

When I think about another visit down that scruffy Harahan back street to Seither's, and I find myself doing just that more and more, I am struck by the unexpected convergence of exigent circumstances, inventiveness, resolve and karma it seems to take to elevate a commonplace neighborhood café into a restaurant worthy of a pilgrimage across a city renowned for its eateries.

In a way, it's like a lightning strike in that you know it happens, you've seen it happen, but you know the odds are long that it will ever happen to you. But it happened for Jason Seither and if you're willing to wander a little bit out of your way, you'll be rewarded with the chance to savor its power.

Seither's Seafood
Neighborhood Casual
279 Hickory Avenue, Harahan
Lunch through dinner, Tuesday – Friday
Dinner only, Saturday
Visa and MasterCard Honored
No reservations
Telephone: (504) 738-1116
No website

Tujague's

What if the drab, slimy gray chunks of cheap meat that appeared upon my plate really would have been considered the zenith, the apogee, the crowning point of Nineteenth Century culinary art?

They very idea that Tujague's could possibly be closing after 156 of operation was unthinkable to hordes of New Orleanians, at least until they stopped and thought about how many years it had been since they had personally dined at the city's second oldest restaurant.

Suddenly, however, city residents were faced with the all too real possibility that not only was Tujague's about to close after the February 2013 death of its owner for the previous thirty years but, perish the thought, the venerable restaurant was about to be replaced by a T-shirt shop and a fried chicken joint.

The hue and cry were loud and sustained, and it wasn't confined to the city. An editor compadre who had expatriated himself to New York City advised me he was one step shy of undone when he heard the news.

There was little question that Tujague's glory days were behind it. People hadn't routinely sat down to the restaurant's fabled seven-course lunches for nearly a century. The world in which Tujague's had once flourished was gone. One of the restaurant's two signature dishes, shrimp remoulade, had gone from unique to ubiquitous in New Orleans. The other, boiled beef brisket with horseradish sauce, had become a culinary curiosity from a bygone age. The rooms had become shopworn if not downright shabby. To say the clock had run out on Tujague's was charitable.

The owner's son hadn't given much real thought to picking up the mantle and making a go of the old place, at least until the uproar surrounding its potential closing made him rethink the notion. After four months of indecision, he bought out the rest of the family, closed the place for some much-needed sprucing up, reworked the creaky menu and reopened.

I'd peeked in the front door and liked what I saw. It was airy and white and with its starched table cloths and bentwood chairs had a similar Creole bistro feel to Galatoire's or its Uptown counterpart Clancy's.

The revised menu may not have brought Tujague's blasting into the Twenty-First Century, but it at least nudged the restaurant into the latter days of the Twentieth. The stand-up bar on the building's front corner remained virtually unchanged from the day it opened in 1856. That was a good thing, I thought, because I find something reassuring about sipping my Sazerac in a saloon where time is at a standstill and the downsides of debatable progress are held at bay.

Indeed, prior to being spruced up, Tujague's looked more like old working class New Orleans than any other "nice" restaurant in town. The main room's downscale brown paneling was festooned with photos, portraits and assorted memorabilia displayed in a manner that might charitably be called "higgledy-piggledy." The room reflected the restaurant's early days as a chow hall serving hearty breakfasts and lunches to the longshoremen, sailors and stevedores that made the old New Orleans French Market the dockside commercial hub of what was then one of America's fastest growing cities.

Times change everywhere, of course, even in New Orleans, although many people including most natives will agree that the clock tends to tick a little more slowly in the Crescent City than elsewhere. During the 159-year run of Tujague's the French Market has evolved from its status the city's premier produce and fish open market into a tourism-driven community bazaar peppered with boutiques and what amounts to a row of food outlets that would be perfectly at home in a suburban shopping mall's food court. Pushcarts have been replaced by diesel-powered trucks. Ladies with sun-shielding parasols and shopping baskets have been replaced by vacationers sporting shorts and clicking pictures with their iPhones. The dozen or more Sicilian grocery stores standing cheek-by-jowl have dwindled down to one that has survived only because tourists line up, often out the door, for a muffuletta, the iconic New Orleans sandwich that was created on premises in 1906.

It amazes me that Tujague's lasted as long as it did with so few changes until 2013. Over the years, it played host to Presidents Roosevelt, Truman and Eisenhower and France's Charles DeGaulle. Notables and celebrities from John D. Rockefeller to Harrison Ford have signed the guestbook as well, but Rockefeller has been dead 78 years and Ford turns 73 in 2015.

That changes were necessary there can be little doubt, and indeed changes were made, but they seem to be slapdash and inconsistent, as if the new owner went with his first impulsive instinct without entertaining a second deliberate thought

People with a penchant for culinary history may want to visit today's Tujague's for no other reason than to experience the last fleeting vestiges that remain of banqueting blue-collar style in bygone New Orleans. Beyond that, I can think of no other reason with the exception of the saloon that greets visitors when they first enter the double doors opening diagonally onto the corners of Decatur and Madison Streets.

It's a long bar, said to be the longest in New Orleans in fact, handsome, sturdy and fashioned out of cyprus with nary a barstool in sight. While modern times have made it more common to see tourist sneakers than work boots on the foot rail, it remains the kind of bar people "belly up to," have a pop or three and leave rather than linger.

The back bar is dominated by an ornately framed mirror of epic proportion that looks to be in the neighborhood of ten feet square. Impressive enough in size as it may be, the mirror grows in stature when one considers its provenance. When it arrived from France in 1856, it had already seen ninety-six years of service in a Paris Bistro dating back to the reign of Louis XV and a time when Marie Antoinette was a three year-old toddler in Austria.

Perched at the bar with my foot hiked on a rail, I have found myself contemplating the engineering, dray horse and manpower it must have taken to move 100 square feet of brittle glass through the streets of Paris by wooden-wheeled cart to a square-rigger crossing the choppy waters of the North Atlantic, up the Mississippi River and finally across the cobblestone streets of the French Quarter before affixing it to a saloon wall where it would reside without a scratch for the next 159 years. Such daydreaming is, at least to me, far more engaging than watching Clydesdales trudge in endless circles around an electric beer clock.

It is not difficult for one to set back their mental clock to the 1860s and envision men hoisting cut-glass schooners of tap beer from bung-popped barrels or firing down shots of redeye or sipping New Orleans' beloved "green fairy," absinthe, from demitasse cups made of bone china. Yet most people, this author included, are surprised to find out that one of the world's most enduring cocktails, the minty green Grasshopper, was first concocted on the famous cypress bar in 1928, during the depths of Prohibition, by Tujague's owner Philibert Guichet, Jr., as an entry for a New York cocktail recipe contest (it came in second, or so the story goes).

If, once one enters the double doors of the front bar at Tujague's, today's realities fade into the mists of a history that never was or merely may have been, going through the saloon's back door into the restaurant can produce the equivalent of an abrupt slap.

The service may not have been as a bad as a perusal of interactive tourism websites suggest, but when we were left cooling our heels in a dumpy foyer while our server, after looking directly at us, turned her back and walked out the restaurant door to continue a call phone call, well, it was a less than auspicious start.

Our empty water glasses were filthy, so we asked for new ones. A busser looked around several other tables inspecting glasses in the light to try and find clean ones. After producing two that weren't much cleaner than the originals, he started to pick up empty glasses from other tables to take back to the scullery while the server, finally off her cell phone, vociferously cussed about the ineptitude of the previous night's staff.

The butter for our French bread was a frozen briquet wrapped in gold aluminum foil, no sin perhaps in a hash house, but a cringe-worthy faux pas in a restaurant that sells its fare based upon Old World traditions of elegance and grace.

Having come into Tujague's to dine on their vaunted beef brisket, the selfsame item that had produced torrents of nostalgia from my editor buddy marooned in New York, I was not about to let an accumulating list of minor sins deter me from what I had been assured was an epicurean equivalent of Nirvana on a plate.

I should have known better.

I really, really should have.

In recent years, the lowly beef brisket has been elevated by the stable-to-table crowd from a cut of meat so cheap it was the chuckwagon staple of cowboys, whose only other dinner option involved a hundred mile horseback jaunt through sagebrush, into a hoity-toity cut so gushed about by New York fooderati that its price is beginning to nudge the lower end of premium steak. This year's hyperbole aside, it's still a tough, stringy cut of second-tier beef that doesn't tenderize until it's been in a pot about the same length of time it takes to parboil a 300-pound missionary in a cannibal's cauldron.

What the kitchen presented to me were four chunks of stringy, grayish brisket that had been boiled without benefit of salt, pepper or any semblance of spice of human thought. On the side was the house tomato-based horseradish sauce, which tasted suspiciously like seafood cocktail sauce, and had obviously spent the evening nestled up against the frozen butter briquets that had earlier emerged with the French bread.

While I've had worse meals in New Orleans (I'm almost sure I must have), I can honestly say I've never experienced anything so bland, boring and banal in any restaurant, anywhere, that claims to have preserved the pinnacles of cooking tradition from the Golden Ages of a more refined and genteel past.

But as I write these words, a thought occurs. What if the kitchen at Tujague's is right and the rest of the world is wrong? What if the drab, slimy gray chunks of cheap meat that appeared upon my plate really would have been considered the zenith, the apogee, the crowning point of Nineteenth Century culinary art? If Brillat-Savarin's maxim, "Show me what you eat and I'll show you what you are" is true, does this explain why the world we have inherited from our ancestors is such a cesspool?

Barbed but deserved criticism of Tujague's aside, the saloon is a great stand-up bar in the sense that a great man is often referred to as a stand-up guy. It's a manly kind of place, at once a little rough around the edges, but at the same time the kind of room where a fellow is expected to act like a gentleman instead of a scoundrel.

But be aware that the Age of New Orleans Grace ends at the saloon's back door, where the owner might consider posting a sign – from Dante – saying, "All hope abandon, ye who enter here."

Tujague's
Creole
823 Decatur (at the corner of Madison Street)
Lunch and dinner daily
Reservations accepted and credit cards honored
Telephone: (504) 525-8676
Website: www.tujagues.com

A DOZEN
DAMNED GOOD
PLACES
TO DRINK

It has been said, in fact often slurred, that there are more saloons per capita in New Orleans than anywhere else in the United States and quite possibly the world.

I don't know anybody who's made it to all of them. My pal, Slider Bob, told me of a time years ago when he and a buddy decided to start at one end of historic St. Charles Avenue and stop in every saloon that had the word "lounge" on it. When asked how far the pair got on their quest, Slider told me they couldn't remember, but swore it had to be at least three blocks.

New Orleans has worked to build its reputation as a two-fisted drinking town, and what the local residents haven't managed to accomplish on their own, they've been fortunate enough to have millions upon millions of visitors come riding to their rescue.

For generations of Southern frat boys and co-eds, it has been a veritable rite of passage to drink enough ruby red, sicky-sweet Hurricanes at Pat O'Brien's in the French Quarter to empty their stomachs into the storm drains on St. Peter Street.

In 1984, during the New Orleans World's Fair, a newer, higher octane cocktail called the "Hand Grenade®" was introduced at the Tropical Isle, a two-story tourist Mecca on the corner of Bourbon and Orleans Streets. The melon-flavored concoction of God-only-knows-how-many liqueurs comes in a green plastic glass, which has grown into an iconic emblem of the shitfaced visitor.

Despite the wretched excesses of the Hurricane and the Hand Grenade, New Orleans is, for the most part, a civilized drinking town.

It has been claimed that the cocktail itself was invented in the city around 1830 by an enterprising pharmacist named Antoine Amédée Peychaud, whose bitters remain an integral part of the city's hard cocktail culture.

Over the years, all manner of cocktails have been invented behind the cypress bars of the city's saloons. The Sazerac, Ramos Gin Fizz, and Grasshopper all got their start in New Orleans and that heritage of mixology is still alive and well in numerous craft cocktail watering holes around town.

In a city devoted to pleasures of both the flesh and spirit, visitors don't have to go very far before they find their kind of bar. New Orleans has a little bit of everything, from elegant lounges with grand pianos to dive bars, LGBT clubs, neighborhood pubs and music venues where the music is jazzy and the barkeeps pour hard.

In assembling this collection of a dozen damned fine places to drink, I've avoided writing about places whose sole raison d'etre is to get college students and less than circumspect visitors drunk enough to drop their guards, drop their inhibitions and drop Heaven only knows what else.

Because there is no earthly way to winnow all the city's superlative drinking establishment down to a definitive dozen best, I've tried to offer a cross-section of places where a pleasure-loving populace gather to, as they say in New Orleans, "pass a good time."

Yes, it's one of the world's best jobs, but the best part about it is that it's a job that's never, ever, finished.

Cheers.

A DOZEN DAMNED GOOD PLACES
TO DRINK

Napoleon House

*Taking a look around the main bar room in the front of the building,
one easily gets the impression that changes have been few, if any, and that over
the past century, the total expenditure on decorations might approach twenty bucks.*

Napoleon House is more of a saloon than a restaurant, but
more than that, it is perhaps the city's ultimate exemplar of democracy
in action.

It's not uncommon to see local residents in business dress and
tourists sporting flip-flops and Mardi Gras beads at adjacent tables
blithely ignoring each other in a laissez faire environment that is more
advertised than realized in "the city that care forgot."

In truth, many New Orleans residents have conceded their
beloved Vieux Carré (the French Quarter) to the masses who make
tourism one of the city's largest industries. Beyond an occasional foray
to such bastions of the city's old ways as Galatoire's and Antoine's, or a
visit to see why people are buzzing about a new chef on the block, many
locals have come to regard the Quarter as a place to bring company from
out of town before returning to the relative equanimity of their own
neighborhoods.

With the city's carefully cultivated image as a hotbed of decadence,
drunkenness and debauchery, it should not surprise anyone when the
French Quarter becomes a magnet for visitors far from home intent on
giving their repressed hometown behavior a test drive or, at the very least,
watch others try their hands at the wheel. In fact, it can be argued that
before Las Vegas unleashed its randy "what happens in Vegas stays in
Vegas" advertising campaign, New Orleans was widely regarded as America's "sin city." Considering such a pedigree, it's not difficult to see why

local residents keep a wary eye on tourists; nor should it come as a surprise that their outings into the Quarter are commonly infrequent.

Yet in the heart of the packaged prurience of the French Quarter, a mere two blocks above Jackson Square on Chartres Street, is this oasis of civility, gentility, and tranquility. And to many people, resident and visitor alike, there is no other place that typifies New Orleans as does the ramshackle bar that, were it in any other city, would be a likely candidate for the wrecking ball.

The 200-year-old building was originally the home of mayor Nicholas Girod, whose term in office (1812-1815) overlapped the historic Battle of New Orleans. A loyal Bonapartist, Girod offered his house as a home to Napoleon, who was in his second exile on the island of St. Helena, 1200 miles west off the African coast in the middle of the south Atlantic. Legend has it that Girod was trying to hatch a plot to spring Napoleon from captivity when "the little corporal" up and died, rendering the entire enterprise theoretical.

In 1914, the Impastato family opened their bar and restaurant in the building, where it has been in operation ever since. Taking a look around the main bar room in the front of the building, one easily gets the impression that changes have been few, if any, and that over the past century, the total expenditure on decorations might approach twenty bucks. The plaster and paint have nearly disappeared, often replaced by overlapping strata of graffiti. Paintings, posters, and photographs go from fading to yellowing to thoroughly obscured by a thick brown patina arising from decades of heat, humidity and smoke.

French doors open off the St. Louis Street side of the bar room providing a view of one of the city's most notorious slave exchanges, and on pleasant days, wobbly tables and rickety chairs inch their way through them to start forming an impromptu sidewalk café, where time slows and the temptation of one more final cocktail keeps the ringside seats from turning over at a Twenty-First Century clip. Mules pull carriages filled with tourists past the St. Louis Street tables and someone listening closely to the patter of the coachmen will learn a different history of the building over the rhythmic clopping of hooves with the passing of each coach.

In the midst of the city where jazz was cradled, American gospel planted its roots and a joyous Cajun zydeco beat now pounds out the front of trinket shops, Napoleon House is a defiant anachronism. The music in the bar room is big boy classical — a thundering Beethoven symphony one minute, Pavarotti powering through a Puccini aria the next — and there is a fundamental rightness to the music that is undeniable. In nearly forty years, I've never heard anyone have the temerity to suggest switching it to rock, funk or (God forbid) country. It's as if a cantankerous specter stands sentry in the room, ready to advise a musical philistine that there are several dozen other places in the Quarter that play the new stuff and the door is in the corner.

One thing missing from Napoleon House, but not really missed at all, is the ubiquitous display of photographs of people both famous and infamous who have frittered away an hour or a lazy afternoon going all the way back to the year Archduke Franz Ferdinand was shot dead in Sarajevo and the world plunged into war. While many places cover their walls with pictures of presidents and popes, silent stars of the silver screen or television's talking heads, the lack of same at Napoleon House tacitly implies that this is an egalitarian saloon, one where the owners don't give a damn who you are as long as you have enough money to buy a drink and the common sense to leave everyone else alone.

The specialty drink at Napoleon House is the Pimm's Cup, actually invented in England in 1840 and more traditionally associated with Wimbledon and afternoon cricket matches, a cooling blend of Pimm's No. 1 gin-based liqueur and three ounces of lemonade topped off with 7UP and garnished with cucumber. No one seems to know exactly how or when the Pimm's Cup became the saloon's liquid mascot, but in a place that takes yesteryear's events at face value, no one really needs to. Some things are just the way they are, period.

In 2014, Napoleon House eased into its second century as a bar with a minimum of fanfare. The Pimm's Cups continued to pour, the pictures continued to age, and when jaded residents happened to make eye contact with wide-eyed visitors there may even be a few quick nods of recognition. But in a New Orleans that continues to change, who

could possibly want Napoleon House to change along with it?
Raise your glass to democracy at its best. Hear, hear.

Napoleon House
500 Chartres Street, (at St. Louis Street)
Monday, 11:00 a.m. -5:30 p.m.
Tuesday – Thursday, 11:00 a.m. – 10:00 p.m.
Friday – Saturday, 11:00 a.m. – 11.00 p.m.
All major credit cards are accepted, but no reservations
Telephone: (504) 524-9752
Website: www.napoleonhouse.com

Arnaud's French 75

*In a city that can be as boisterous as New Orleans,
the bar at Arnaud's is conducive to hushed conversations.*

Within two years of its being founded in 1918, Arnaud's restaurant and accompanying saloon were threatened with extinction by the passage of the Volstead Act, which plunged the nation into thirteen years of Prohibition.

Most New Orleans restaurants surviving the "whisky drought" did so with a wink and a nod, and Arnaud's was no exception, serving bootleg hooch in coffee cups while local law enforcement officials looked the other way.

When Prohibition ended and business-as-usual returned, Arnaud's was one of the several restaurants that started pumping its money into immediately neighboring real estate. Buying a building at a time and connecting the rooms with labyrinthine passageways, the proprietors transformed what appeared to be normal-sized restaurants, judging by their exteriors, into a maze of dining rooms with enormous capacity. Today, Arnaud's is a complex of a dozen different dining rooms, while Antoine's weighs in with fourteen.

Oddly enough, one of the loveliest rooms in Arnaud's is a bar, which has a separate entrance and is called the "French 75." With its deep wood panels, beveled crystal, playful monkey lamps, elegant combination of settees and comfortable chairs, the room remains evocative of America's pre-Prohibition era. It is a saloon straight out of the age of grand hotels, an illusion further enhanced by its menu of both contemporary craft and New Orleans classic cocktails.

While I'm sure one of Arnaud's top-notch bartenders would serve me a cold beer in their bar room, and no doubt do so graciously, I'd feel silly ordering anything less than a Sazerac or perhaps a classic martini.

In a city that can be as boisterous as New Orleans, the bar at Arnaud's is conducive to hushed conversations. Whether by design or merely serendipitous happenstance, the room is an oasis from the hurly-burly of the raucous end of Bourbon Street roughly fifty yards from its brass-handled doors. Even on the occasions when chat gets particularly animated and a gale of laughter erupts from one of the dozen or so tables in the elongated room, it remains one of the more civilized saloons in all of New Orleans and certainly the French Quarter.

Like most of its fellow "grand dame" restaurants in the city, Arnaud's has had to reluctantly change with the times. Jackets are encouraged for gentlemen, but no longer required. I believe shorts and blue jeans are discouraged, but after our recent visit, it's hard to say. Indeed, the world is a far more casual place than it was ten years ago, let alone one hundred.

That isn't to say that attention to one's wardrobe or appearance is a thoroughly lost custom. At heart, New Orleans in many ways remains an Old World enclave where many patrician natives continue to show respect to the institutions serving them by dressing for cocktails before dinner in one the city's classic restaurants. And while it is perhaps a matter of age, I find myself far more comfortable blending in with those who revere the old ways of their venerated institutions than taking up with those who would downgrade them.

Arnaud's certainly has its flaws, some of them brought on by its attempt to remain a bastion of civilization in a city supported by hordes of people trying to escape it. But the flaws are minor, the criticisms bordering on the hairsplitting. Most importantly, when you find yourself standing in the middle of the insanity of Bourbon Street thirsting for relief, it's refreshing to realize that civilization is just around the corner.

Arnaud's French 75

813 Bienville at Bourbon Street

Monday – Thursday, 5:30 pm – 11:30 pm

Friday and Saturday, 5:30 pm – 12:30 am

Sunday, 10:00 am – 2:30 pm

All major credit card accepted

Telephone: (504) 523-5433

Website: www.arnaudsrestaurant.com

Samuel's
The Blind Pelican

As someone who doesn't so much get a craving for a flawlessly chilled platter of raw oysters as an out-and-out jones, this is the equivalent of catnip to a calico.

I can think of any number of good reasons to visit The Blind Pelican, one of the more cheerful casual restaurants and saloons along a stretch of St. Charles Avenue near Lee Circle that harbors plenty of both.

The raised terrace beside the bar and the sprawling patio amid shade tress at street level are two of the better places to kill a sunny afternoon or starry night when the weather has been ordered up by the Chamber of Commerce.

It's like someone re-thought the entire notion of a fern bar and decided to do it right and, more importantly, in a way that would make it fit into New Orleans instead of a shopping mall.

There is one reason, however, that lifts The Blind Pelican from being a good place into a great bargain. During happy hour from four until eight every afternoon of the year, the place serves a dozen oysters on the half shell for three bucks with every cocktail you order.

As someone who doesn't so much get a craving for a flawlessly chilled platter of raw oysters as an out-and-out jones, this is the equivalent of catnip to a calico.

I am of an age and era that I can still remember when it wasn't all that uncommon to find saloons running ten-cent oyster specials. One of the great discoveries of my life may have been a ramshackle beachfront joint on the Florida Panhandle that offered two-dollar dozens with frosty Miller High Life longnecks for a quarter. While such a once idyllic world may have fallen prey to hurricanes, oil spills, red tides and runaway inflation, being able to reclaim at least a small slice of it on St. Charles Avenue is nothing less than manna.

Since there's no reason to string adjectives about oysters on the half shell, considering there isn't any real difference between one and the next and people either love or loathe them, suffice it to say they're presented in the traditional manner and with the usual complement of sauce, horseradish and lemon wedges.

The stipulation, of course, is that the price is based upon one dozen, per adult beverage, per person. To that end, there is a full bar in addition to thirty-four local and international draft beers, most of which lean toward craft breweries.

One doesn't expect dirt-cheap oysters to be served with heavily discounted drinks and they certainly don't at The Blind Pelican. While the prices won't rival what can be found at the hundreds of corner bars peppered across the city, they're generally less than the amount you'll be set back in a hotel with at least two stars.

As you might imagine with three-dollar dozens, The Blind Pelican can get relentlessly busy and at times chaotic, but the people of New Orleans love their oysters and they're just as crazy about an almost unbelievable deal.

Get 'em while they're cold.

Samuel's The Blind Pelican
1628 St. Charles Avenue (at Euterpe Street)
Daily 11:00 am – 2:00 am
Telephone: (504) 558-9398
Website: http://www.theblindpelicanbar.com

Cosimo's

With its location in the lower end of the French Quarter,
visitors thinking "Bourbon Street" are in for a gentle awakening.

It's been over fifty years since the assassination of President
Kennedy, perhaps the single largest source of conspiracy theories ever,
and the story keeps swirling around that the plot was hatched in the back
room of a New Orleans saloon.

Maybe it's true. Maybe it isn't. Anyone who knows is most likely
dead, and if they aren't, it's pretty obvious they're in no hurry to talk
about it. At any rate, here's the fact, if indeed it is a fact, and you can
decide for yourself if it's true, if it's bunk or if you even give a damn.

The bar is Cosimo's, a generally quiet watering hole in the lower
French Quarter about two blocks in from Esplanade Avenue, the street
generally recognized as the end of the city's most famous historic district.

Myth, legend or whatever, it's said that the Kennedy assassination
was plotted in the back room of Cosimo's by none other than Lee Harvey
Oswald himself. If that's true at all (and that's a Texas-sized if), depending upon which conspiracy theory is being promoted at any given time
on late-night cable television, the co-conspirators could have had the
back room packed with Mafiosi, Cuban mercenaries, Soviet KGB agents,
the FBI, Southern segregationists or even Lyndon Johnson (although I
suspect someone would have looked up from their seat at the bar and
recognized the Vice President of the United States when he walked in).

Now I have no idea whether there was a fiendish plot and it was
hatched in the back room of Cosimo's, but I've always been a sucker for

a good yarn, so I decided to walk the two blocks from my apartment at the time and check it out for myself.

I liked Cosimo's immediately.

I think the main reason was that there wasn't anything tricked up about the place.

The beer is cold, the help is friendly and it's nice enough without being trendy, self-conscious or tragically hip. In my mind's eye, it's the kind of bar where you stop on your way to dinner for a cold one, more of a way station than a destination.

As for the vaunted back room, where the crime of the century is reputed to have been planned, well, it looks like something out of an aging East Coast frat house. There's a pool table in the center and scattered furniture that's seen better days. At first glance, it looks far more likely to have been the scene of a keg party than a shadow-cloaked conspiracy. Come to think of it, it still does at second glance. And third.

Cosimo's dates back to 1934, the year after "The Noble Experiment" was declared a failure and Prohibition was cleared off the books. With its wood-paneled walls and ceiling and several unremarkable chandeliers, it was perhaps a little swankier than it looks more than eighty years later. The back bar, with its columns, beveled mirrors and whisky cases tucked behind harlequin-glass doors, suggests that Cosimo's was once a tad more elegant, or at least had pretentions of it, than the quiet neighborhood watering hole it is today.

With its location in the lower end of the French Quarter, visitors thinking "Bourbon Street" are in for a gentle awakening. The location at the corner of Burgundy and Governor Nichols Streets is one of the more quiet areas of the city's most notorious districts, an area where people experiencing the Quarter for the first time start saying to themselves, "Yes, I could live here," at least until they see the real estate prices.

While Cosimo's gets a certain amount of visitor traffic due to its location, it is primarily a hangout for local residents. You'll see a lot of Bloody Marys being served, not so much because it's a brunchy kind of restaurant, but rather because they have a hard-earned reputation for serving one of the better Bloody Marys in a cocktail-fueled town.

In my forty-plus years of being above the legal drinking age, I have graduated from the noise and grime of the Bourbon Street maelstrom to the gentle nine-to-five vibe that may not be as good for tourist business but is less fraying upon the nerves of its residents. To that end, I find myself dropping by Cosimo's when I'm in the quiet end of the Quarter.

Cosimo's is not the Mardi Gras, voodoo, continuous parade, and anything-goes New Orleans that most people come to expect if they watch enough TV. Rather, it's the New Orleans that city residents try to quietly preserve for themselves. And as any conspiracy buff knows, the most successful conspiracies are built out of silence.

Of course, you never heard this from me.

Cosimo's
1201 Burgundy Street (at Governor Nicholls)
Monday and Tuesday, 4:00 pm - 2:00 am
Wednesday – Friday, 4:00 pm - 5:00 am
Saturday, 2:00 pm - 5:00 am
Sunday, 2:00 pm - 2:00 am
Telephones: (504) 522-9715
No website

Orleans Grapevine

Ultimately, the Grapevine is an eminently likable saloon.

Over thirty years ago, someone came up with the bright idea that sticky-sweet, ruby red Hurricane cocktail served by the legendary Pat O'Brien's saloon wasn't potent enough. Never mind the fact that the Hurricane had proven itself to have a remarkably emetic effect upon several generations of college students, but no, someone had to build a bigger bomb.

Ah, science.

The mixologists at a Bourbon Street saloon, once challenged, were more than up to the task. Blending God-only-knows-how-many liqueurs and who knows what else into a melon flavored anti-sobriety weapon they proudly named the Hand Grenade®. Proudly proclaiming it the "most powerful drink" in New Orleans, they trademarked the name, cloaked the formula in commercial secrecy and used their considerable marketing budget to warn that they were the sole guardians of the flame and offer rewards to anyone who would rat out lowlife imitators.

The whole thing is rather silly, of course, from the trash-the-tourist competition between Tropical Isle and Pat O'Brien's to the neon green plastic cup, shaped like a grenade, that at least is visible enough from across Bourbon Street to serve as fair warning that potential trouble may be staggering in your direction.

And, yes, I'm jealous as hell over the money the owners of the Tropical Isle must be piling into a Brink's truck every day at sunrise.

Over the years, the Hand Grenade has grown from its sole location at the Tropical Isle and can now be found (fully licensed, of course) in about a half dozen saloons on or around Bourbon Street. It's been joined by such other creations as the Shark Attack, Tropical Itch, Horny Gator and others.

Personally, I can think of few things worse than to be trapped in a Bourbon Street saloon on the other side of midnight, pouring neon potions for people whose sole aim is knee-walking, commode-hugging drunkenness. It would add a tenth hellish circle to Dante's Inferno, and I always wondered what the people behind all this revelry did for fun.

Until I found out.

It seems that several years ago the owners of Tropical Isle decided to open an intimate wine bar and bistro one-half block down Orleans Avenue from their flagship Bourbon Street location. The reason, so I've been told, is they wanted a place where they could go and quietly drink what they liked instead of what they sold. If that's indeed true, I can't say I blame them.

Orleans Grapevine is a study in hushed understatement. From its half-dozen sidewalk café tables, it opens into a U-shaped wine bar with a few assorted tables scattered around the room. The unobtrusive, usually elegant music comes from an unmanned, Internet-driven player piano. The room is classic New Orleans interior brick with an ornate wine cage running along the entry wall. In the far end of the room, a doorway leads to a cozy courtyard bistro, the menu of which skirts the fine line separating fussy/trendy and downright pretentious.

The only hint of Orleans Grapevine's scrupulously unmentioned provenance is a table tent card on the bar promoting their Hand Grenade Martini, a ghastly incongruity in such an oasis of civility.

In the spring of 2014, Orleans Grapevine added a wrinkle that was at once trendy, insidious and clever as hell. During happy hour, which runs from 4-6 p.m. and 10p.m. until midnight Monday through Friday, an event featuring some better than passable wines for five bucks a stem, a separate wine glass brimming with complimentary crisp bacon slices materializes along with your drink order. It's a cunning touch, saltier than peanuts or pretzels, far better suited to wine and cheese and a distinctive signature for a room built as an antidote to the frenzy of its surroundings.

Ultimately, the Grapevine is an eminently likable saloon. On a pleasant evening, the café tables along Orleans Avenue, with their location exactly halfway between the bacchanalia of Bourbon Street and the serenity of the St. Louis Cathedral gardens, provide some of the quirkiest people-watching in the city.

While the wine bar can get pricey, like any other good wine bar in a major city, it is a friendly enough place to while away a late and lazy afternoon with gratis bacon and respectable pinot noir.

About the only thing missing is a Hand Grenade in a neon green plastic cup, and one look at the French Quarter regulars surrounding the bar will tell you that no one is missing that very much at all.

Orleans Grapevine
730 Orleans Avenue
(Between Bourbon and Royal Streets)
Open daily from 4 p.m.
Telephone: (504) 523-1930
Website: www.orleansgrapevine.com

Laffite's Blacksmith Shop

*To be fair, the Blacksmith Shop has — or at least had —
a certain scruffy charm about it.*

Laffite's Blacksmith Shop is often dubbed as the oldest bar operating under one roof in America, dating back to 1722 or 1723. No one's quite sure.

It's said to have earned its name from notorious pirate Jean Laffite and his brother, who supposedly used the old brick-between-post building as a front for their illegal activities. But no one's quite sure.

Legend has it that brothers Laffite hid their treasure of piratical loot somewhere in or under the building. Over the centuries, people have dug, looked for secret passageways, and chipped away at the masonry, all with no luck. But again, no one's quite sure.

Are you beginning to see a pattern emerge?

Well, this is probably what you should expect in a building where people have spent the last several hundred years spinning whoppers while sipping everything from cognac to Coors Light.

In truth, New Orleanians love the stories more than they love the Blacksmith Shop, which they demonstrate by staying away in droves.

To be fair, the Blacksmith Shop has — or at least had — a certain scruffy charm about it. It remains one of the most photographed buildings in New Orleans, even in the wake of an amateurish exterior "restoration" more suitable to a miniature golf course than a historic landmark.

External aesthetics and local desertion aside, Laffite's Blacksmith Shop is still a damned good place for a drink, particularly in the afternoon. Because minimal electric light has been added to the building and its thick exterior walls, the bar's open windows opening out onto the more quiet end of Bourbon Street frame the mule-carriages that routinely stop in front of the place while their drivers revise, rewrite and generally mangle the history of both saloon and city.

On sun-dappled days when the Chamber of Commerce has commandeered the weather, a lazy drink in the coolness provided by the thick walls has a way of turning into another, and perhaps another after that, accompanied by the clopping hooves of mules. Rainy days transform the dark interior into a cave you won't want to leave.

In the evenings, a courtyard awaits out a side door. At night, people encircle a grand piano to take a crack at singing old standards with sometimes surprising, sometimes unspeakable results. It's a holdover from the 1950s through the 1970s when the bar hosted a predominantly gay clientele, one that is said to have often included Tennessee Williams, although it has been suggested he was more spectator than participant.

Today, Laffite's Blacksmith Shop caters mainly to tourists, conventioneers and visitors of all stripes. While its location is on the outer edge of New Orleans' largest LGBT area (sporadically referred to as "Below the Lavender Line") the crowd has become, for want of a better word, more "mainstream." Just the same, diehard homophobes would probably be more comfortable in other establishments.

Gawking can prove a daunting challenge at Laffite's. The room is mainly lit by candles on the small number of tables. There is a big blue jukebox in the corner and the ubiquitous television to break the conspiratorial mood one hopes for in a place like this. Beyond that, lighting is minimal at best; some service lights behind the bar, electric lights in the otherwise dark bathrooms and some lights around the piano.

While there's a full line of beers and mixed cocktails, it seems the most common drink I see is the dreaded Hurricane, reputed to be superior to those purveyed by Pat O'Briens, and a purple drink I've only referred to as "that purple drank," both of which are served in that greatest of New Orleans inventions – the plastic go-cup.

The simple truth about Laffite's Blacksmith Shop is that minus the history and what little authenticity remains of its architecture, the joint would be just another dive bar with a historic address. Minus the tourist trade, it would be either boarded up or another Bourbon Street condom boutique.

Oddly enough, however, despite its numerous flaws, from surly service to its apparent eagerness to class down for a lower common denominator, it can be a most pleasant place to sit at an open window and watch "The World According to Bourbon Street" stagger by. I know. I've been there more often than I care to admit.

Laffite's Blacksmith Shop Bar
941 Bourbon (Between Dumaine and St. Philip Streets)
Daily, 10:30 a.m. — 3:00 a.m.
Telephone: (504) 593-9761

Website: www.lafittesblacksmithshop.cpm

Buffa's Lounge

*What's so noteworthy about Buffa's is that there's really
nothing all that noteworthy about it.*

A guy walks into a bar dressed as a crab (the guy, not the bar).

Spying an albino mongrel snoozing on the floor, the crab shrieks,
"Hello, Pinkie-Winkie! You know me, Mr. Crab!" Several guys turn
from the football game on the TV to see what the hell is going on.
Pinkie-Winkie snarls and snaps at Mr. Crab, who starts backing out the
door. The guys go back to their football game.

It's another Sunday afternoon at Buffa's, a downscale bar in front
with a casual, upscale music hall in the back. Located on Esplanade Avenue across the street from the lower end of the French Quarter, it's
nigh on impossible to say what Buffa's is beyond, "It's New Orleans."

Dating back to 1939, Buffa's always has been and continues to be
a work in progress. Menus change. The emphasis shifts between music
and whiskey. Lately, the décor has changed, brought on by a continuing
squabble with a truculent guy who bought a house next door to the established New Orleans music venue and promptly proceeded to belly-
ache about the volume. Despite its continuous evolution, Buffa's has
never strayed very far from its original mission, namely, to be a neighborhood bar and a pretty damned good one at that.

What's so noteworthy about Buffa's is that there's really nothing
all that noteworthy about it. On the ceiling, there's a double fan that
looks like it might have been part of an old DC-3 prop plane in a former
life. Beyond that, Buffa's is your basic B-flat saloon.

The long bar isn't littered with tent cards ballyhooing fluorescent novelty cocktails. The folks working behind it are friendly enough, but don't make any real effort to chat you up. You order your drink, get it, drink it, pay and leave. A quick glance around the room reveals more longneck beer bottles than cocktail glasses. Ultimately it's a bar for working people and on that basis it works just fine.

The front bar is open 24/7, and there's always someone in the kitchen, cranking out breakfasts, bar munchies, and some predictable New Orleans entrees. The back room runs on a much more limited schedule.

Some fifty or sixty years ago, there was a local guitarist of some note, name of Mack Rebennack, who had a part of his fretting finger shot off in a fight. In order to keep his blossoming career as a professional musician going, Rebennack allegedly spent hour upon hour in the back room of Buffa's, emerging at the end of it as one of the top keyboard artists in New Orleans, a city highly regarded as one of the world's great piano towns. Today, the world knows Rebennack better (and you probably do, too) as Dr. John.

Throughout 2014, Buffa's served as the reluctant centerpiece of a long-brewing feud between musicians and club owners on one side and proponents of a city ordinance to limit decibel counts in music venues on the other. It's a dispute that has been going on for years, featuring city ordnances, hearings, revised city ordinances, unresolved litigation, still more revisions to the laws, mediations and, as you might imagine, continuing revisions.

From the sidelines, it becomes fairly apparent that neither side will be entirely happy with the outcome, assuming one is ever reached. Nonetheless, in its effort to be a both responsive and responsible neighbor, Buffa's has added new soundproofing, baffling systems and sound-absorbent wall coverings to its back room at cost substantial enough it was forced to conduct a public fundraising event to defray the considerable expense.

While Buffa's is not immune to the vagaries of a changing New Orleans, the seventy-five year-old saloon hasn't changed all that much. It's always been the neighborhood bar "on the border of the Quarter," and never seems to have given any thought to becoming anything more.

If you're in town looking for a cold one, here's a bit of advice. Don't go to a bar that runs ads in tourist magazines claiming they're "where the locals go." For over three-quarters of a century, Buffa's has been a hangout for some of New Orleans' most colorful characters. Just ask Mr. Crab and Pinkie-Winkie.

Buffa's Lounge
1001 Esplanade Avenue (at Burgundy Street)
Daily, 24/7
Telephone: (504) 949-0038
Website: www.buffasbar.com

Markey's Bar

*It's still an old-school corner bar that appears
to have blithely ignored the changing neighborhood around it.*

THIS IS A MEN'S BAR.
FEMALES ARE TOLERATED ONLY
AS THEY REFRAIN
FROM EXCESSIVE TALK.

I don't know how old the sign on the mirror over the back bar is. It does-n't look old, tattered and faded enough to have come from an era where it would have been posted with anything but a tongue planted firmly in cheek.

Just the same, Markey's still embodies the boisterous spirit of an Irish-American bar with its roots rebelliously planted in 1925, the mid-dle of Prohibition. While New Orleans has more than its share of tra-ditional Celtic-Irish saloons, Markey's Bar is emotionally closer to Boston than Ballybunnion.

In recent years, the Bywater neighborhood where the bar has al-ways been, has seen real estate prices skyrocket as more artists and ur-banites were pushed downriver from the French Quarter through the Fauborg Marigny. Today the neighborhood has the shabby gentility that comes through gradual gentrification. It's now a district with an explod-ing number of hip, trendy cafes, bistros and watering holes nestled among the shotgun and bargeboard houses of what was once a truly blue-collar neighborhood.

Fortunately, none of this seems to have had any effect on Markey's. It's still an old-school corner bar that appears to have blithely ignored the changing neighborhood around it. The diagonal doors at the corner have been bolted shut for years. These days the nondescript entrance is halfway down the side of the red bargeboard walls. Walk in and you're roughly halfway down a surprisingly long bar with eighteen barstools lined down the side. There are a few chattering televisions, a handful of raised café tables and conventional four-tops.

Looking to the right there's a small cluster of stools and more raised tables leading into a semi-open kitchen. The limited food service is Any Bar, USA; burgers, wings, couple of fried baskets, a hot dog, quesadillas, some poor boys, the usual suspects.

Look further to the right, down the inside door of the place, and you'll the most talked about feature of the entire joint. It's an old-fashioned bar shuffleboard machine, not one of those truncated jobs designed to save space, but the real deal designed to serve as the centerpiece of the saloon. Near as I could tell, it's at least twenty feet long, perhaps more, the only seeming concession to modernity being a digital scoreboard suspended over the middle of the puck sliding lane.

It's a slow Friday when my pal, Piñata Boy, and I wander in. Three couples are seated outside at metal tables enjoying Chamber of Commerce weather. Four tolerated females are at the customer side of the bar, seemingly mesmerized by the more than two dozen beer taps in front of them. (It should be noted that they are speaking in low, non-excessive tones.)

Once their order has been served, the two of us order and I start chatting up the convivial bartender, a fellow who appears to be about forty and says he's been there about fifteen years. He tells us the place has been owned by the Markey family since the 1940s, but he doesn't know who owned it before that, or what the name of the place was. I notice an old political sign for a "Michael Markey" taped to the mirror on the bar back. Judging by the haircut and wardrobe, it looks like it probably dates back to the early 1960s, the Kennedy era.

One of the things I've noticed and liked over several trips to

Markey's is that, while it's definitely a neighborhood bar where the vast majority of people are regulars, there's not the standoffishness that seems to be the occupational hazard of corner taverns everywhere. The people at Markey's are genuinely friendly, and if they're not all Irish, and they certainly all aren't, well, let's hoist a few in the name if international harmony.

In a neighborhood that's spoiling to elevate its demographics, it's refreshing to discover a saloon that refuses to be spoiled along with it.

Markey's Bar
650 Louisa (at Royal Street)
Daily, 11:00 a.m. — 2:00 a.m.
Telephone: (504) 943-0785
No website

The Spotted Cat

*You won't find a morsel of food in the place, just booze and music;
there's no real need for anything else.*

It should come as a surprise to no one that in a city with as vibrant and
historic a music culture as that to be found in the Crescent City there
would be a wealth of venues dedicated to everything ranging from alternative to zydeco.

Clubs, music and dance halls run as wide in styles as musical styles
run deep, but the roots of jazz run deeper in New Orleans than anywhere else in the world. Jazz was invented in the city, and while it has expanded beyond its wellsprings of brass marching bands and bordello
pianos, it remains as easy to enjoy traditional New Orleans jazz as it is to
dig into a plate of red beans and rice at high noon on any given Monday.

Over the years, old time jazz has moved from its origins in the
city's Storyville red light district and expanded citywide, but today the
heart of the New Orleans music scene beats along five blocks of Frenchmen Street, just beyond the lower end of the French Quarter. Most of
the clubs are smaller and tend to be funkier than their Bourbon Street
brethren, offering an intimacy harkening back to the times when popular music, particularly jazz, was more commonly associated with vice
rather than virtue.

In a city where picking a restaurant for dinner can quickly escalate
into heartfelt arguments about the relative merits of the cuisines of com-
peting kitchens, it's not surprising that local residents are equally passionate about their clubs. With that caveat placed squarely on the center

of the table, I keep finding my partiality growing for one of the more modest clubs on the street.

That place is The Spotted Cat. You won't find a morsel of food in the joint, just booze and music; there's no real need for anything else.

A converted storefront, The Spotted Cat's limited geography commands intimacy from players and patrons alike. The L-shaped bar, which seats about a dozen, and the postage stamp of a stage tucked behind the front door take up half the club, leaving a haphazard seating and standing room area for about twenty-five or thirty patrons depending upon their feelings about togetherness. Despite such crowded conditions, its not uncommon to see three or four couples dancing, in fact quite often jitterbugging, in front of the bandstand.

Beyond the eccentric geography, the décor such as it is falls somewhere between spare and eclectic. There are about a dozen pieces for sale from local artists, a white conduit sculpture of three musicians, the name of the club painted on the wall and several signs around the place advising customers of a one drink per set minimum.

Drink prices are acceptable for a club that generally has no cover charge and a tip bucket is passed around with some but not excessive regularity. Cash is the only coin of the realm accepted, and there is an ATM in the back for customers finding themselves cash-stripped after being caught up in the action

The music at "The Cat" is as eclectic as everything else about the joint. There are always two acts, and more often three, every night, and they don't seem to have the first shred of thematic continuity behind them.

Case in point. On a recent visit, when we entered a group that for lack of a better term might be called an alternative/blues/rockabilly acoustic quintet was playing for a youngish crowd sporting substantial numbers of tattoos and piercings. As they packed their gear, they were replaced by the Orleans 6, a traditional Dixieland jazz band that has held the 6 PM Wednesday slot for the past five years. While the bands changed, so did the audience. By the time the Orleans 6 hit the downbeat on

"Muskrat Ramble," the house was noticeably gray at the temples and expanding at the midsection.

While the music seems to be constantly changing, The Spotted Cat seems to feature a small yet steady progression of bands ranging from washboard blues and female swing trios to a tattooed chanteuse backed by a hot brass section. The house website is both helpful and kept current for patrons unwilling to take their chances on the club's menu of musical pot luck.

With its tattered intimacy and eclectic lineups, The Spotted Cat isn't merely one of the city's more authentic jazz clubs, it's also one of the best

The Spotted Cat
623 Frenchmen Street (Between Chartres and Royal)
Open Monday – Friday, 4:00 pm – 2:00 am
Saturday and Sunday from 3:00 pm
Telephone: (504) 943-3887
Website: www.spottedcatmusicclub.com

The Apple Barrel

Like it or not, the watchword at The Apple Barrel is "togetherness."

Two doors down Frenchmen Street from The Spotted Cat is The Apple Barrel, not only one of the smallest bars in New Orleans, but so small that the very idea of musicians actually playing there borders on the absurd. But play they do, in defiance of the laws of logic, geography and no doubt the city's blithely unheeded fire ordinances.

The Apple Barrel sits on the ground floor of a rickety building roughly the color of orange sherbert, beneath a nearly invisible but equally ramshackle gem of an Italian bistro named Adolfo's. The stairway running upstairs from the separate entrance to the restaurant is clearly visible but its ornamental cage makes up the entire left wall of the downstairs club.

The club's entrance doubles as a music venue, which feels more like an afterthought than a bandstand. Music is quite often a solo guitarist, sometimes enhanced by a singer, although I've seen photos where three people have somehow managed to shoehorn themselves in and still leave room for patrons to come and go.

Like it or not, the watchword at The Apple Barrel is "togetherness."

The four tables in the place are barrels, presumably apple but more likely whiskey, making the six chairs in the room more likely candidates for intense games of musical chairs than perches from which to appreciate the efforts of the cramped musicians. The twelve barstools wedged around the L-shaped bar provide the opportunity for customers to make new acquaintances on a cheek-to-cheek basis. In the small area between the barrels and the bar is enough space to pack perhaps a dozen or so more revelers, providing they keep their elbows tucked close to their ribs.

A number of years ago, The Sensible One and I watched a block-long jazz funeral procession for a notable player leave St. Louis Cathedral and make its way toward the Apple Barrel, where an impromptu jam session purportedly broke out.

Using New Orleans music club logic, six chairs, twelve barstools and standing room for a dozen means The Apple Barrel has a comfortable occupancy capacity of about sixty, not counting special occasions like jazz funerals where it almost certainly triples.

As bars go, there's nothing special about The Apple Barrel. A quick scan of the place indicated that more people appeared to have their fists wrapped around longnecks than were drinking cocktails. Whether that's because the smallish bar back simply lacks the capacity to hold a lot of hooch or it's more of a beer joint by customer preference I can't tell, but I couldn't help but notice the beer cooler in the puny pantry behind what passes for the bandstand was packed to the gills while the bar shelves weren't.

Ultimately, The Apple Barrel is a polarizing saloon. Its combination of minimal real estate and maximal compression lead some people to hate it with the same intensity with which others love the joint. The funny thing to me is that I can't decide which camp I fall into. I guess The Sensible One and I will just have to keep going until we can come to a decision.

The Apple Barrel
609 Frenchmen Street (Between Royal and Chartres)
Sunday – Thursday, 1:00 pm – 3:00 am
Friday – Saturday, 1:00 pm – 5:00 am
Cash only
Telephone: (504) 949-9399
No website

Molly's at the Market

Most importantly, it's one of the most unassuming Irish pubs in New Orleans,
clearly not impressed with itself or, for that matter, you.

I know I've seen Monaghan behind the bar a hundred times, but it seems the urn containing his ashes has finally gone missing.

On second thought, maybe it hasn't.

Everything else in Molly's at the Market seems to be in place. The sarcophagus is still wedged between the ceiling beams over the short end of the bar. The taxidermically preserved alligator, head defiantly raised, continues to gather dust on its elevated platform next to the rusting six-shooters. The traffic light randomly blinks in the rear corner.

I'm sure Jim Monaghan's remains still have to be somewhere in the saloon he founded so long ago. Some Irish bars gain character as they age, others acquire a mellow patina, but Molly's accumulates enough clutter to hide almost anything. Then again, considering the number of pranksters who wander in and out of Molly's, some joker may have swiped, moved or otherwise hidden old Jim.

You must understand, Molly's at the Market is not so much iconic as it is playfully iconoclastic. Located on the lower end of Decatur Street in a part of the French Quarter that seems to be a magnet for runaways and drifters, in its forty-plus years Molly's has emerged as the anchor on the strip of straightforward watering holes that line the 1100 block.

During Katrina, Molly's was said to have been the second French Quarter bar to open, beaten to the punch only by Johnny White's on St. Peter (which never closed at all). It's the unofficial center of the French Quarter's St. Patrick's Day celebration, when it is overrun with local celebrities serving as guest bartenders to legions of gawkers. Most importantly, it's one of the most unassuming Irish pubs in New Orleans, clearly not impressed with itself or, for that matter, you.

Molly's is deceptively small with four long tables running down one wall and its bar running down the other. At the front of the place is what The Sensible One and I agree is one of the best tables in the city. It's an open window with a counter and two stools opening onto Decatur Street. In a city where people accept the more joyful forms of insanity as business as usual, it's ringside on where not only anything can happen, but if you sit there long enough, most of it will.

Between the front door and the counter facing the street is an old jukebox overseen by a large poster of a grim-faced Pope Pius XI. Why he's there no one is quite sure, but there's something paradoxical watching him scowl as Neil Diamond tunes warble out of the jukebox below the pontiff's ceremonial vestments.

Among the memorabilia scattered around and above the bar room are well over a dozen signs from restaurants, bars and coffee houses that have gone belly up over the decades. Looking around, I can't help but wonder if the owners of the failed establishments brought the signs in as they came to drown their sorrows or if, over the years, Monaghan et al went scavenging. Either way, the remains of so many broken dreams and dwelling upon them can draw me into waves of wistful nostalgia on a sunny day to a brooding Irish melancholy when it's pelting rain and cold beyond the balcony.

Much happier is a mocked-up highway sign, with white letters on Interstate green, advising that Iowa City is two miles down the road while Molly's at the Market lies a short 969 miles away. Having gone to college less than 28 miles from Iowa City myself, the sign particularly tickles my funny bone. And that attitude may explain why I take particular delight in the many, many hours I've spent on barstools or gazing out the open counter window at Molly's over the past forty years.

Between its mix of hardcore neighborhood regulars and occasionally over-served vacationers there's always something going on and it's often ridiculous to see. Look up or around and you'll see something

181

new or quirky that may or may not have been at Molly's last week. And despite the wistful reminders of other closures, the old girl still keeps an Irish twinkle in her eye and a ready wink for the throngs of thirsty newcomers who belly up to the bar.

Even though I haven't seen Monaghan behind the bar in a while, he's there in spirit if not flesh or ashes. Hoist one to the old boy.

Molly's at the Market
1107 Decatur Street
(Between Ursulines and Governor Nicholls)
Daily, 10 a.m. – 6:00 a.m.
Telephone: (504) 525-5169
Website: www.mollysatthemarket.net

The Crown & Anchor

Call the pub what you will: quirky, slightly cantankerous, off center, left-handed, slightly behind the times or a hotbed of English eccentricity.

Owen would be happier if someone had the good manners to put another pint of Guinness stout on the bar in front of him. He doesn't have any money and his half-sister, Lizzie, is out cold on the floor beneath his barstool.

None of the regulars lined up along the bar at The Crown & Anchor are paying any attention. They're all used to Owen's routine and it's come to the point that his begging no longer works.

It may be a dog's life, but it's okay, considering that Owen is a border collie with a stray or two somewhere in his bloodline. Besides, he and Lizzie have already been able to cadge a pair of meat sticks out of the barkeep.

One of the great traditions in New Orleans is that of dog-friendly accommodation in taverns not offering on-premises food service, and The Crown & Anchor is widely regarded as one of the most welcoming. There's almost always a dog or two in the authentically English pub, and I've seen the inventory run as high as eight pups of varying breeds and temperaments ranging from mastiffs to Mexican hairless.

As far as anyone knows or the regulars are willing to admit, The Crown & Anchor is the only certifiably English pub in a city brimming with Irish saloons. Publican Neil Timms is an affable ex-pat from Coventry with a culinary school education and rigid adherence to the traditions of Mother Country's pubs and alehouses. His wife and partner Albena, born and raised in Bulgaria, ladles on a dollop of Old World conviviality and warmth.

For visitors, getting to "the Point," where The C&A is tucked away, can be as much fun as first spying the blue Tardis that leads into the pub's corner door. The Point is Algiers Point, which was founded in 1719. It's the second oldest settlement in Louisiana, having been established two years after New Orleans. Now a part of the city itself, the Point is across the Mississippi River from the French Quarter and the best way to get there is by pedestrian ferry

The plat of land itself is more or less rectangular, roughly a mile across and a half-mile deep, and two of its four sides are nestled below the levee that kept the historic neighborhood dry during and in the aftermath of Hurricane Katrina.

At the foot of Canal Street on the city side, next to the Aquarium of the Americas, you'll find the entrance to the Canal Street Ferry. It's not much of a ride, taking maybe ten minutes to chug across the Mississippi River to the West Bank. The terminal, particularly on the New Orleans side, is a depressing specimen of municipal architecture. An industrial, institutional pile, the first thing the terminal makes me think about is how out of place it looks in a city devoted to pleasures of the senses.

Once you board the ferry, make your way to the uncovered end of the boat. It seems that even on days when the heat covers the city like a wet wool blanket, there's still a breeze on the mighty Mississippi, and as the wind tousles your hair, you have the opportunity to lean against a rail and behold one of the better views of the city. The historic French Market and the triple spires of St. Louis Cathedral define the Vieux Carré, and to the left rise the towers of downtown.

A bevy of ships pass by, from barges to tankers to cruise ships, and even the sternwheeler Natchez glides past with the stately grace of a wedding cake on the waters with her rolling paddles and out-of-tune steam calliope. It's a surefire way to start feeling truly connected with the 300-year history of New Orleans and the river that has forever been her lifeblood.

Over time, the Point has been a railhead, home to shipyards, slaughterhouses, naval stations and even the Civil War powder magazine for her sister city. Until the "Crescent City Connection" bridge was completed in 1958, the Point was most accessible by the ferry and remained a small and sleepy town. That small town character remains today, and one can walk atop the levee around the tightest bend in the Mississippi River, look one way and see a shimmering cityscape, then look the other direction into a neighborhood dotted with Victorian Era housing and an unforeseen number of steeples.

It's a gentle life. Informal. You won't find many neckties or see many legs wrapped in pantyhose. The neighbors often refer to themselves as "Algerines."

Once inside the historic village, it's easy to forget you're less than a half-mile from the pulsating heart of New Orleans until you see the high-rise buildings across the river peeking over the top of the levee. The levee works to muffle most city noise. Beyond the bellowing of ships' horns, the neighborhood's most common sounds are dogs barking and the peal of church bells.

Even though the community inside the levee is Kansas flat, it doesn't feel that way due to tree-lined streets and a collection of residential styles that cause a constant nodding of visitors' heads as they take in the panoply of architectural details, inviting porticoes, ornamented rooflines and vibrant colors of a bygone era. With a history squarely footed in the Eighteenth and Nineteenth Centuries, Algiers Point presents a mélange of homes ranging from cozy bungalows and Creole cottages to the occasional stately Victorian sandwiched into a line of traditional New Orleans "shotgun" houses.

Less than two blocks from the ferry terminal on the West Bank, The Crown & Anchor fits hand-in-glove with its surrounding village. Call the pub what you will: quirky, slightly cantankerous, off center, left-handed, slightly behind the times or a hotbed of English eccentricity. If you're as blessed as The Sensible One and I were in 2014 to trade our visitor status for permanent as Algerines, you'll soon call The Crown & Anchor the same thing we do: home.

For a small pub (12 barstools and six mostly smallish tables), it's surprisingly well-stocked with whiskies, brew taps and the ability to mix off-the-wall cocktails, such as the "Timm's Cup," which is pubkeeper Timm's combination strong variation/weak pun on the classic British Empire Pimm's Cup.

Entertainment at the C&A is mostly comprised of conversation and darts. When the Dr. Who television program runs original episodes on Saturdays, the place's two television sets draw an eager cult of fans. A projector TV is brought in for New Orleans Saints games. Occasionally, small bands are impossibly shoehorned in front of the pub's normally out-of-tune spinet piano. Pub quiz trivia events are occasionally held on Thursdays. As befits the temperaments of C&A regulars, events are sporadic and often spontaneous.

In the cherished tradition of English pubs, The Crown & Anchor is as much the heartbeat, message exchange and nerve center of its village as it is a tavern. Like any other grog shop where regulars gather, it may take more than a single visit to become "part of the furniture," but Neil and Albena will see to it that your welcome is warm, your pint is the right temperature and your leaving will be filled with a determination to return.

Once you do, when you see Owen at the bar, don't throw him a bone. Buy him a Guinness and you'll have made a lifelong friend. Cheers.

The Crown & Anchor
200 Pelican Avenue in Algiers Point
Sunday – Thursday, 11:00 a.m. – 12:00 a.m.
Friday and Saturday, 11:00 a.m. – 2:00 a.m.
Telephone: (504) 227-1007

Website: www.crownanchorpub.com

Acknowledgements

First and foremost, thank you.

Special thanks to my dining companions, drinking pals, running buddies and cheering section: Banker Bill, Ginger Babe, Marlboro Man, Piñata Boy, Slider Bob and "Yeaux, B!" Your identities remain protected to spare you guilt by association.

Thanks to my intrepid publicist, Kelsey McBride of Book Publicity Services, for warning over 400 media outlets and restaurant blogs that yours truly is up to his old tricks again.

Most important of all, my heartfelt thanks to The Sensible One, Lil McKinnon-Hicks, my tireless editor, conscience, crying towel, lover, bride and sidekick, for making a joyous generation of meals in New Orleans taste better than any man deserves.

About the Author

Novelist and recovering ad man Steven Wells Hicks spent forty years driving 192 miles up and down Interstate 55 between Mississippi and New Orleans, loving every minute coming south and loathing every second going back north. Buoyed by the success of his 2014 novel, *Destiny's Anvil*, he and The Sensible One pulled up stakes and now make their permanent home in New Orleans' Algiers Point Historic District.

19673169R00109

Made in the USA
Middletown, DE
29 April 2015